Elementary 4-5 Book Two
Color and Composition

Written by Brenda Ellis
Edited by Ariel DeWitt
Developed by Brenda Ellis and Daniel D. Ellis
Illustrations on pages 50, 56, and 61 by Daniel D. Ellis
Other illustrations, all photos, and cover art by Brenda Ellis
Student artists are acknowledged beside their works as they appear in the text.

Third Edition

ACKNOWLEDGMENTS

Thanks to my husband, Daniel Ellis. Thanks to editor, Christine Ann Feorino for her wonderful suggestions on the first edition of this book. Thanks to those students who let us share their work with others through this book. Thanks to Dover Publications Inc., NY and Art Resources, NY for supplying the fine art images by the great masters.

Copyright © 2000, 2008, 2013 by Brenda Ellis
All rights reserved. No portion of this book may be reproduced – mechanically, electronically or by any other means, including photocopying. Don't compromise the educational value of this book by photocopying images. Children cannot see what a painting should look like when color and tonal values are reduced to black and white.

Printed in the U.S.A.

ISBN 978-1-939394-05-7
Published by
Artistic Pursuits Inc.
Northglenn, Colorado
www.artisticpursuits.com
alltheanswers@artisticpursuits.com

Getting Started

Page	Unit	CONTENTS
2		Contents/Art Supplies
3		What Parents Want to Know
		Book Content and Scheduling
4		What Students Want to Know
		The Mysterious Language of Color
5		Color
6	1	Color Wheel
11	2	Primary Colors
16	3	Secondary Colors
21		The Elements Combined- Sketch, Color, Paint
22	4	Intermediate Colors
27	5	Tinting and Shading
32	6	Neutral Colors
37		The Elements Combined- Soft and Hard Edges
38	7	Values of Colors
43		Composition
44	8	Direction and Movement
49		The Elements Combined- Shapes and Textures
51	9	Rhythm
55		The Elements Combined- Blending Colors
56	10	Front and Back Points of View
61	11	High and Low Points of View
66	12	Emphasis of Details
71	13	Buildings
76	14	Figure
81	15	Face
86	16	Interiors
91		Evaluation Sheet
92		Bibliography

ART SUPPLIES

1 - watercolor pencil set of 12 (Derwent or Prismacolor suggested)
*1 - Prismacolor colored pencil set of 12
1 - #8 watercolor brush round
1 - watercolor paper pad
1 - sketch pad for drawing
1 - vinyl eraser
1 - metal handheld pencil sharpener

*For the dry technique lessons in the second half of this book the watercolor pencils can be used dry or a set of Prismacolor Colored Pencils can be purchased.

ADDITIONAL ITEMS: drawing board, can or jar for a water container, masking tape, paper towels, tracing paper.

Getting Started

What Parents Want to Know
Book Content and Scheduling

To learn to make art in color artists have always focused on two groups of topics known as color theory and principles of design (composition). Each unit in this book introduces one of these topics over four lessons. Each topic is explored in unique ways, giving students enough experience with the topic that they naturally incorporate it into the way that they draw or paint. It becomes part of their thinking as they draw any kind of subject matter. This kind of focus, and ample opportunity to practice, is how children learn to make art in color.

First Lesson of Each Unit

Building a Visual Vocabulary

Here students are given a topic to focus on explained in words and pictures. The creative exploration assignment guides students to observe the topic in their own environment. They make connections to real-world experiences, and create a work of art from their own observations and ideas. The assignment for this lesson is colored blue.

Second Lesson of Each Unit

Art Appreciation and Art History

Students see how the topic is used in a work of art by the masters and apply their new observations to a work of art that they create. Students gain knowledge of artists and art history. The assignment for this lesson is colored blue.

Third Lesson of Each Unit

Techniques

Students learn how to use the materials and tools of art and apply that knowledge to make an original work of art. The assignment for this lesson is colored blue.

Fourth Lesson of Each Unit

Application

Students do a final project incorporating new techniques and application of the topic while using a variety of references such as still life objects, landscapes, portraiture, photographs and more! The assignment for this lesson is colored blue.

Scheduling Art Class

CLASSES PER WEEK: TWO   **TIME PER CLASS: ABOUT ONE HOUR**

This schedule can be modified to fit yours. Keep in mind that students can work independently so it is their time you are scheduling, not your own. Schedule art class at a time when they can complete the art assignment, even if it runs over an hour. Once interrupted, students can rarely return to an activity with as much enthusiasm as they first had. Time for completing each activity will vary greatly depending on students' approaches; however you should see that as they learn to use more of the elements within their pictures that they are taking more time on each piece.

What Students Want to Know
THE MYSTERIOUS LANGUAGE OF COLOR

If the secrets of color were contained in a book, would you open it? We hope your answer is YES! Just as learning the rules of a sport adds to your enjoyment of playing it, learning the rules of color adds to your enjoyment of making art in color. The first thing everyone should know is where to find the rule book for color. The rule book is the color wheel.

1. Learn the rules of color using the color wheel.

"OK", you say, "I'm looking at the color wheel and I don't see any rules." We won't let you be stuck there. Each unit in this book will introduce you to the vocabulary of the color wheel. As you practice one idea at a time, you will soon understand how to mix any colors you want with the few that are in your color set. The second and most important secret when dealing with color is all about what set you choose. Choose a set that contains blue, red, and yellow as shown on the color wheel. Most sets that are designed for students will contain the primary colors that you need.

2. See color variations and color mixtures.

Your brain is a storehouse of color knowledge. You would agree that oranges are orange and lemons are yellow. Each statement has simplified what we really see in order to reduce it to one color for easy identification. What we really see are reflections, shadows, color combinations, and all kinds of other factors which change the original color. Artists learn to see these color variations and color mixtures. An orange may appear blue in the shadows. A lemon may appear green around the ends.

3. Exaggerate colors

Artists may overstep the bounds of truth when applying color to the paper. They do this in order to make objects clearer and easier to identify. They might exaggerate to create a mood. They might use color for its associated meanings by using red because it seems "hot" or green because it seems "peaceful". By using the color rules you will unlock the secrets of color and gain the skills to work in color with confidence.

Getting Started

COLOR

Color completes the study of the elements. Here are a few things to know about color before you start.

PIGMENT

Pigments are the source of color for our paints. Some pigments are man-made, but many are made from minerals, animals, and vegetables. The substances are crushed into a fine powder.

BINDER

People have found a variety of ways to bind the powder together to make a substance they can work with. Binders can be oily or sticky substances gum arabic, eggs, or oils from plants. Regular types of color pencils use a binder of wax.

FILLER

Fillers, like plaster, are often added to art supplies. Fillers lessen the intensity of the pigment. Cheap products often have far too much filler to give satisfying results. More expensive supplies have less filler so that one is able to get more color out of them.

WET MEDIUM

When a pigment and a binder are mixed together so that the results are a liquid we say it is a wet medium. Paints are wet media. The pigments are suspended in the oil or gum and water binder. The first section of this book will introduce you to watercolor pencils. They have a binder of gum Arabic that dissolves when mixed with water. It acts like watercolor when wet.

The sample above was applied with a watercolor pencil, and then brushed with water.

DRY MEDIUM

When a pigment and a binder are mixed together we get a medium. When mediums are mixed so that the result is a hard substance like a crayon, color pencil, pastel, or chalk, we say it is a dry medium. When you use colored pencils without water you use a dry medium. The second section of this book will introduce you to dry medium techniques.

The sample above was applied with a wax-based Prismacolor pencil on drawing paper.

Lesson 1

unit 1
color wheel

Vocabulary and Creative Exercise

The color wheel is a useful tool that shows how colors relate to each other. By using a color wheel you can learn how colors work together and why certain color mixtures turn out as they do. Artists, interior decorators, and advertisers use the color wheel. Look at your watercolor pencil set. Which colors on the color wheel do they most closely match? Are there colors in your set that are not found on the two color wheels such as brown or gray? In the next seven units you'll learn how each color is part of the color wheel or is made from mixing colors on the color wheel.

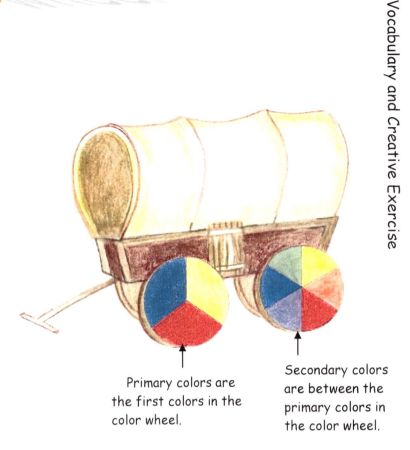

Primary colors are the first colors in the color wheel.

Secondary colors are between the primary colors in the color wheel.

using creativity

Some activities are relaxing and lead to creative thoughts. Look into the sky and watch the clouds go by. Watch a thunderstorm approach. Stand in a crowded place and watch the people. Watch fish swim in an aquarium. When you take time to watch simple things your mind can sort, rearrange, invent new ideas, and create new solutions.

TRY IT: Find an activity that you can watch, preferably outdoors, while letting your mind wander. Watching T.V. is a distracting activity and not recommended. After a time of relaxed watching, pick up paper and pencils. Draw what you see.

OBJECTIVE: to relax and observe so that new information can be accumulated, processed, and used for creative purposes.

Look at Color in Art   Lesson 2

Our world is full of color and we may not think much about it until we see a beautiful sunrise or leaves suddenly turn from green to bright yellow in the fall. When artists make a painting, they create a little world with color. Albert Bierstadt created a sunset view of a wagon party in the painting, *The Oregon Trail.* In this painting the clouds are orange, purple, and gold on a blue sky. From far away the mountains appear purple, orange, and blue. Even the trail appears orange and gold. We can become more aware of color when we see how artists like Bierstadt used it.

Albert Bierstadt, *The Oregon Trail*, 1869. 31 x 49 in. Photo Credit: Dover Publications Inc., NY

While we might think a mountain peak is brown and a sky is blue, look at the colors Bierstadt used.

Purple
Orange
Gold

Many of the colors seen in the sky are reflected on the mountain cliff.

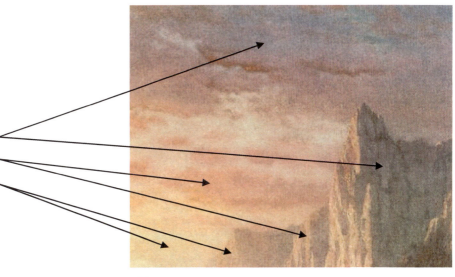

Art Appreciation

7

THE ARTIST:
Albert Bierstadt (1830-1902)
American Landscape Painter

Albert Bierstadt was the son of a barrelmaker. We can guess that his interest in art started in childhood because at the age of twenty he displayed thirteen works in Boston. Boston was the art center of America at that time. Bierstadt went to Europe for additional training, as most American artists were expected to do. At age twenty-nine he traveled to the territories of Colorado and Wyoming with the United States government survey expedition. Surveyors made maps of new territories. When he returned to New York he made large scale paintings from the sketches. He became well known in the nation and in the world as a New World landscape painter.

MAKE AN OBSERVATION PAINTING:
Draw a sketch of a landscape. Use watercolor pencils and brush areas with water to blend them.

THE TIMES:

Imagine the excitement of discovering a whole new world with unique animals, river systems, waterfalls, mountains, hills, and wild weather patterns. This is the type of excitement felt by the nation and the world as Americans began to explore the continent from the east to the west in the first half of the 1800's. "Landscape paintings were more popular with nineteenth-century Americans than with any other people in the Western world. The great American wilderness was part of their daily life..." (Batterberry 80). Artists of the Hudson River School were some of the first to explore and paint the scenes. They did not rely on photography, a fairly new invention, but made sketches in the wild territories and then came back to civilization and their studios to paint large canvases. Many landscape paintings of this time are a mix of truth and imagination. They express the awe of the viewer. These paintings were influential and made people want to move west.

When using a brush do not smash it. Use the tip for a thin mark, or press down a bit for a wider mark as shown.

When you finish painting always rinse the brush in cool water. Press the hairs to a point. Store the brush upright in a jar.

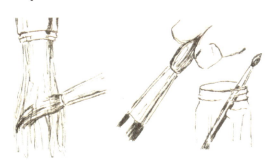

Lesson 3

How to Use Watercolor Pencils

Watercolor pencils are a great bridge from the dry medium of pencil to the wet medium of watercolor. The process of using them is done in two steps.

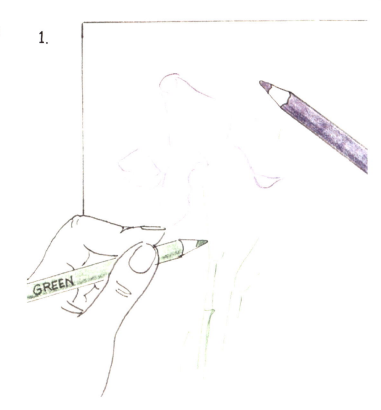

1.

1. DRAW

Draw outlines onto watercolor paper with watercolor pencils.

2. PAINT

Dip a brush in clean water. Pull it across the water jar's edge to take out excess moisture, and then apply the wet brush to the line drawing. To prevent water puddles from collecting on the paper, dab the brush onto a paper towel to pull water from the brush. When using a brush, always pull it across the paper. Never mash the bristles flat against the paper. You can use the point of the brush or the middle section.

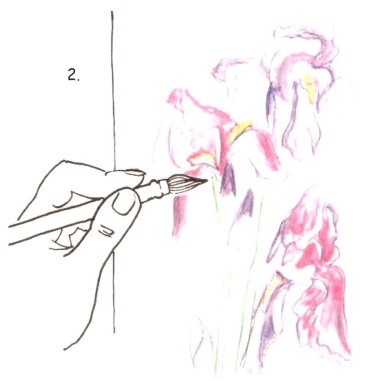

2.

SOMETHING TO TRY: Choose a subject. Draw it using watercolor pencils. Add water with a brush as shown.

Final Project Lesson 4

Application

Look at a landscape. You can look at something outside your window or get a picture of a landscape from a calendar or other visual source. Paint the landscape. Look closely at colors and choose watercolor pencils that you think best match what you see. The colors may look different in the pencil than they do on paper. Test pencils on a piece of scrap paper to see how the colors will appear in your picture.

Organize your tools. Place the paper directly in front of you. Tape the edges to a drawing board or to the table surface with masking tape. This will keep the paper from curling when it gets wet. Place the brush, paper towel, and water on the right side if you use your right hand to paint. Place them on the left side if you use your left hand to paint. The pencil set can be placed above the paper.

YOU WILL NEED

- watercolor pencils
- watercolor brush
- watercolor paper
- water container
- paper towels
- drawing board or table surface
- masking tape

Student Gallery

Student work by Maude Darger was painted from a calendar picture.

THE SUBJECT

A landscape can have people and other objects within it. Bierstadt's painting man and a variety of animals. You can include cars, people, animals, or other subjects you are interested in.

LOOK BACK! Why does the subject in your painting interest you? Did you use more than one color in your painting?

Lesson 1

primary colors
unit 2

Vocabulary and Creative Exercise

The primary colors are yellow, red, and blue. They are the first and most important colors on the color wheel. Yellow, red, and blue are very bright when used together, as shown.

using creativity

A familiar object can often be the inspiration for something new. It is said that engineer John Smeaton observed the strength of a tree trunk during a storm. He decided it was the best form for resisting high winds. He designed the first successful modern lighthouse with round sides curving in from the bottom like the oak tree. When people see an object and make something new from it they are using creativity.

TRY IT: Find a small object in nature that looks interesting to you. You may already have a collection of such objects. Study the object carefully as you imagine yourself shrinking and the object getting larger so that you see only a part of it. Draw that part large enough to fill the page. You are exploring a familiar object in a new way, using observation and imagination.

> OBJECTIVE: to see objects with a new perspective and to think about new ways to draw objects that may have more interesting results.

Look at Primary Colors in Art   Lesson 2

One color is rarely seen alone. A color usually stands in the company of other colors. The surrounding colors affect the way we see the first color. In this painting of people at the beach the brilliant primary colors are set against a dark brown background. The artist, Thomas Hart Benton, seems to color the painting in a way so that blue, red, and yellow are sprinkled throughout the picture. With your finger, trace the path of each of the primary colors as they weave through the painting. Some paths we found are shown below.

Thomas Hart Benton. *People of Chilmark (Figure composition)*. 1920.
Photo Credit: Dover Publications Inc.

12

THE ARTIST:
Thomas Hart Benton (1889-1975)
American Realist Artist

Benton was born in Neosho, Missouri to a family of politicians. He spent some childhood years in Washington D.C. while his father served as a congressman. There he observed the great national art works. He especially liked the wall murals in the Library of Congress. In the 1920's and 30's, Benton traveled across the United States sketching in steel mills, logging camps, and cotton fields. He used those sketches for large mural paintings which depicted ordinary people as heroes of America. He showed that the activities of their daily lives helped build a strong nation that Americans should be proud of. Thomas Hart Benton was the leader of the American movement called Regionalism.

MAKE AN OBSERVATION PAINTING!
Choose one color. Practice painting people while they hold still like the figure below.

THE TIMES:

Modern art from Europe at this time became more abstract. It developed out of the disillusionment people felt from the World Wars in Europe and the Great Depression. At the same time America was introduced to Modern art, American artists in the Midwest counterbalanced it by creating realistic work of a new flavor. Most people did not understand what abstraction was about, but the realists used bold colors and simplified figures to make statements that people understood. The two strongest realist groups in America in the early 20th century were the Social Painters and the Regionalists. Social art showed what was happening in American cities. The topics often accused government of injustices to common people and sometimes brought about governmental change for the good. The topics of Regionalism showed what was already good in the country. The art showed a picture of the life Midwesterners led in farming communities. These artists felt proud of the way Americans had worked together during the rough years of the Great Depression, a time when people lost jobs and prices for everything dropped. "No one had anything. We were all in the same boat so we helped each other," recalls one Midwesterner. Grant Wood, Thomas Hart Benton, and John Steuart Curry chose to paint these good-hearted people. Their works were shown together at the Kansas City Art Institute in 1933. A publicist for the museum called this "real American art" that "seeks to interpret American life." Their themes were local cities, farm communities, and the history of America.

Lesson 3

How to Make Hard and Soft Edges

A hard edge is usually used on the edge of the object. Here it is used to show the top of the birds head. The tip of the brush is used to pull a hard edge.

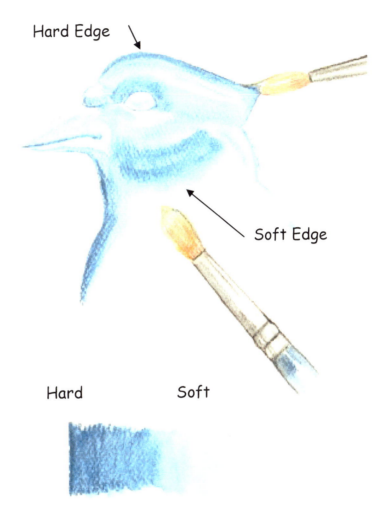

Hard Edge

Soft Edge

Hard   Soft

A soft edge is usually used inside an object to show the form, going from dark to light. Dip the brush in water. Add a bit of pressure to the brush so that its bristles spread out slightly. Pull the brush downward spreading the color evenly throughout the form.

SOMETHING TO TRY: Choose a subject from your room. It may be a toy, a figurine, or a shoe. Make a painting of it using hard and soft edges. Keep it simple by using only one color.

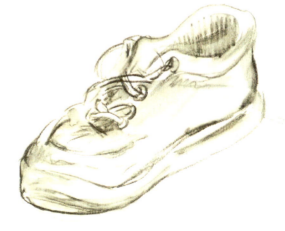

14

Paint a favorite subject from real life using watercolor pencils. Look at the subject as you draw it. Draw onto the paper first, and then paint with a wet brush.

Choosing the subject for painting is an important part of making artwork. We enjoy painting pictures of subjects we like. We like subjects that we know well. Think about subjects that are the most interesting to you.

Final Project Lesson 4

Application

Student Gallery

Student work by Lavendar Huskey is painted while observing a pet iguana.

YOU WILL NEED

- watercolor pencils
- watercolor brush
- watercolor paper
- water container
- paper towels

THE SUBJECT

Use favorite subjects. They can be the small things around you.
- small pets
- models
- action figures

LOOK BACK! Did you look at the subject while you painted it? Did you use hard and soft edges?

Lesson 1

unit 3
secondary colors

Vocabulary and Creative Exercise

When two primary colors are mixed a new color appears. Three combinations can be mixed to make the three secondary colors. On the color wheel, each secondary color is located between the two primary colors it is made from.

using creativity

To create, you need imagination. Imagining is thinking of a picture that is not present or seen in the real world. When you read a story the words describe a scene or picture. In your mind, through your imagination, you picture the scene. This picture is a mixture of your ideas about the world, what is around you, and the words from the story.

TRY IT: Choose a description of a dramatic or interesting scene from a book you are currently reading or have read in the past. Scenes are usually described within a page or two of a book. Read the words again, this time picturing what the scene would look like. Draw the scene as you imagine it. Use secondary colors in your work.

OBJECTIVE: to develop skills in using the imagination, or picturing something new.

16

Look at Secondary Colors in Art   Lesson 2

A secondary color is a mixture of two primary colors. When a painting is based on a secondary color scheme, you will see the three secondary colors: orange, green, and violet (also called purple). This painting of a feast day gathering in a Native American community relies on secondary colors. The artist has used green in the trees and hills, orange in the buildings, and violet in the hills, church building, and ground. The secondary color scheme is bright, cheerful, and used throughout the painting.

William Penhallow Henderson (1877-1943) *Feast Day: San Juan Pueblo*, c. 1921 Photo Credit: Dover Publications Inc.

Secondary colors look vibrant when placed next to each other. See how this is done within just a small section of the painting, then look for other areas where this is used.

Green next to violet

Green next to orange

Orange next to violet

17

THE ARTIST:

William Penhallow Henderson (1877-1943) American painter, architect, and furniture designer.

William Henderson studied in Europe for two years, completing many studies of the Old Masters works. Returning to America, he taught art in Chicago. In his late 20's, he traveled with artist Carl Werntz by train, into Mexico and Arizona. There he completed thirty works which included his first Hopi subjects. Later in life he would live in New Mexico and paint the Hopi tribe's lifestyle and landscapes. These paintings are the ones he is remembered for, as well as many private portraits. He and his wife illustrated *Anderson's Best Fairy Tales*. Many artists in the area illustrated books as well as making paintings. Henderson was one of the first artists to work and live in the area, which quickly become popular as an artist community. He was able to capture the vivid colors of New Mexico. He became a founder of the New Mexico Painters Society.

THE TIMES:

The artists that settled in the New Mexico area in the 19th century embraced the culture of the Native Americans that lived there. They built homes of thatch and mud, called adobe, much like the native tribes. Rooms were small, but added onto, spreading out over time. Furniture was made by artisans from wood and painted in the bright colors natural to the area. William Henderson was an architect, (building designer) and a furniture designer. He designed the Wheelwright Museum of the American Indian, located in Santa Fe, New Mexico. It was built as a place to study the Navajo religion. Today it houses collections that document Navajo art and culture as well as other Native American arts. Henderson based his design on the round hooghan, the traditional Navajo home, also referred to as a hogan (Wheelwright Museum of the American Indian). Today many people visit the Taos and Santa Fe areas to view the art, architecture, and the culture that developed in New Mexico from the beginning of the 19th century to today. They also visit traditional Pueblos and see the arts of the Native American communities that have lived in the area for much longer. Their art includes pottery made from local clay, small carvings, jewelry, and paintings on paper.

MAKE AN IMAGINATION DRAWING!
Paint an imaginary landscape scene using secondary colors. To paint, tape the edges of a piece of watercolor paper to a drawing board with masking tape. Draw a picture and fill in the objects or spaces with color. Dip a brush in clean water. Then brush onto the paper. Blend colors on the paper. Dab the brush onto a paper towel to absorb excess moisture when needed.

Lesson 3
How to Mix Colors

Each color has a mixing strength. Blue is very strong. Yellow is not as strong. Look at the amount of primary color in each cup to see the amounts needed to make a secondary color.

Since you cannot measure the pigment in a color pencil, apply more pressure on the yellow color pencil to add more pigment to the paper. Apply less pressure on the blue color pencil to add less pigment to the paper. Use smooth strokes with even pressure while layering color over color.

The results of color mixing vary depending on the kind of blue or red pencil used. However, your results should be similar to the colors of the leaves shown at the right.

These leaves show an example of what you can expect from watercolor pencils with and without water applied. When water is applied, the white spaces of the paper fill in, making the colors appear brighter.

SOMETHING TO TRY: Practice mixing the primary colors to get secondary colors as shown on this page. Use real objects to observe and paint. You can work from real leaves, if the season provides them, or from apples of these colors. Deep red Jonathan apples have purple shadows, while Granny Smith apples are bright green. Many apple varieties are a mixture of red and yellow.

Set up a still life using real objects from around the house. Use at least two secondary colors in the painting. You could use all three secondary colors. The paintings below are of students' models and stuffed animals.

Final Project Lesson 4

Application

Student Gallery

Aaron Garrison uses dinosaur models to create a painting with two secondary colors (top) while Ariel Ellis uses stuffed animals in a painting with three secondary colors (bottom).

YOU WILL NEED

- watercolor pencils
- watercolor brush
- watercolor paper
- water container
- masking tape
- paper towels

THE SUBJECT

Still life objects may include the following items:

- Houseplants
- Flowers
- Fish bowls
- Cups or dishes
- Food items
- Toys

LOOK BACK! Did you set up a still life arrangement? Did you use a secondary color group?

The Elements Combined: Sketch, Color, Paint

This additional lesson shows how you might make a painting of objects that sit in front of you. These techniques can be used with any objects. Choose your own objects and follow the steps on this page.

Set up the objects directly in front of you. Sketch, while focusing on placing the objects onto the page. Erase when needed. Fill in colors with watercolor pencils.

Add water with a brush to create your painting. Once a color is in the brush you can drag it to other parts of the painting. Pay attention to light and dark areas.

When completely dry, lines can be drawn onto the paper again. The finished painting shows areas of color and colored lines. Both are created with watercolor pencils.

Lesson 1

unit 4
intermediate colors

When a secondary color is mixed with more of one primary it becomes an in-between color called intermediate color. Intermediate colors are located in between each primary and secondary color on the color wheel.

Red-orange

Yellow-green

Red-violet

Yellow-orange

Blue-green

Blue-violet

Vocabulary and Creative Exercise

using creativity

People make at art from their own experiences. In an assignment to draw a horse, one person may draw a black horse surrounded by fences. Another may draw a brown colt, alone, drinking from a pool in a forest. One horse wears armor, while another is saddled. Each person forms different images in their minds because each brings a unique set of experiences to the process of making art. To be creative have the courage to think your own thoughts and tackle each project in your own way.

TRY IT: Look for a picture of a horse or another animal that you prefer. Look carefully at the animal, then away. Imagine the animal in surroundings other than those in the picture and draw the scene. You create the background.

OBJECTIVE: to add personal interpretation to a specific assignment.

Look at Intermediate Colors in Art   Lesson 2

Art Appreciation

A painting becomes more interesting when subtle changes are made to the secondary colors within it. Prendergast uses primary colors of red, blue and yellow in the background buildings. As we follow colors like blue in the water we see a mixture of violet that is blue-violet in the water and red-violet in the dock where people walk. Subtle color changes such as this give more interest to any painting.

Maurice Prendergast (1859-1924) *The Grand Canal, Venice*. 1898-99. Photo Credit: Dover Publications Inc., NY.

Look for intermediate colors within this section of the painting:
red-violet and blue-violet,
red-orange and yellow-orange,
yellow-green and blue-green.

23

THE ARTIST:
Maurice Prendergast (1858-1924)
American Post Impressionist

Maurice Prendergast was born in Canada. When his father's sub-arctic trading post failed, the family moved to the city of Boston within the United States. He worked with a group of artists called The Eight. His themes were lighthearted. His style used dabs and dashes in a similar manner to the Impressionists, but the use of watercolor as a painting medium gave the works a completely different look than when using oil paints. Much of his subject matter included crowds of people.

THE ART:

Most artworks we see in museums are painted in oil paints. Prendergast painted in watercolors, the medium you are using in this book. Look at the painting again. Thin layers of paint called washes are seen on the walkway. The red-violet color in the lower right corner is light and darker in some areas because less water is mixed with the pigment. For white, he leaves the white of the paper unpainted. He dabs the brush onto the paper to make waves on the water. Look for other techniques within his work to use in your own work.

MAKE AN IMAGINATION DRAWING!
Draw a picture of a favorite object or interest you have right now. When you fill in the spaces with watercolor pencils, draw right up to the edges. As you paint, do the same with your brush, so that one edge meets another.

A common mistake is to draw almost up to the edge of an object when filling in the background. The drawing at the left shows too much white space around the banana. The white paper shows between the two colors. The drawing at the right shows off the objects because the artist colored to the edges of the banana and filled in the background space. Think of the white of the paper as a color too. Leave white only where you want white color.

Lesson 3

How to Mix Brighter Colors

When intermediate colors are mixed with colors that sit beside them on the color wheel, the result is brighter colors. We see the result of overlapping these colors in the color groups below.

Techniques

a

b

c

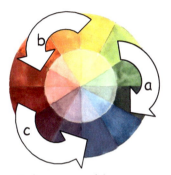

Colors used by themselves mix with the white of the page and are not as bright as they could be. The top row shows the results of using a single pencil found in a set of watercolor pencils. When a second pencil of a different color is used over it, the color appears brighter as shown on the bottom row.

light-green   purple   dark-green   orange   red

light green/yellow   blue/purple   blue/dark green   orange/yellow   red/orange

SOMETHING TO TRY: Practice mixing the colors shown above so that you can see firsthand how your pencil colors mix. Next, make a painting of a bright object using your new discoveries about brighter colors.

25

Draw a picture of something you observe from a photograph. Layer some colors to make them brighter as shown on the previous page.

Student Gallery

Student work above is by Emily Heckman. Student work below is by Hannah Helgeson. Both show rare views of animals. When painting from a photograph we have opportunity to make pictures of animals, which do not usually stay still long enough when working from direct observation.

Final Project
Lesson 4

Application

YOU WILL NEED

- watercolor pencils
- watercolor brush
- watercolor paper
- water container
- masking tape
- drawing board
- paper towels

THE SUBJECT

Draw a scene from a photograph. Photographs can be found in calendar pages, library books, or on the internet. Always have a parent help you find and print out a picture from an internet source. Printing pictures out in a large size uses lots of ink.

LOOK BACK! Did you layer colors that are beside each other on the color wheel in order to make brighter, more intense colors?

Lesson 1

unit 5
tinting and shading

Adding white to a color produces a tint. Adding black to a color produces a shade. Tinting and shading are words for changing the value of a color.

The blue square is tinted.

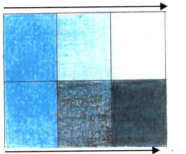

The blue square is shaded.

With color pencils, tinting is done using less pressure on the pencil. Shading is accomplished by increasing the pressure on the pencil or by adding a layer of a darker color or black.

Student work by Ariel Ellis.

Vocabulary and Creative Exercise

using creativity

We tend to quit looking at things that have become familiar to us. We are attracted to things that are new. Objects sitting around our homes become familiar sights to us. We must move them around or we quit seeing them. Sometimes artists have to hunt for new things to see. Artists learn to look at things as if they were seeing them for the first time. You can do that too.

TRY IT: Go to your closet or toy chest and take a closer look. Which objects have interesting shapes for drawing? A worn shoe, broken tennis racket, or the unlaced baseball glove may make good material to draw from. Set an object on the table in front of you. Arrange it so you have an interesting view of it. Draw the object.

OBJECTIVE: to see objects in a new way, as source material for drawing, and to develop eye and hand coordination skills using direct observation.

Look at Tinting and Shading in Art   Lesson 2

Eanger Irving Couse (1866-1936) *Hunting for Deer*, 1909
Oil on Canvas. 24 x 29 in. Photo Credit: Dover Publications Inc. NY

Tinting is making the color lighter. Shading is making the color darker. The light area in this painting of two hunters helps us to focus on the same area that the figures are focused on.

In this scene the area around the two figures is shaded (darker) because they are in the shade of a large tree. The artist, Eanger Irving Couse, in *Hunting for Deer*, knows how to get us to see the deer by tinting one area of a darkly shaded painting.

The deer is centered within the tinted part of the painting as it stands in the open prairie exposed to the sunlight.

Art History

THE ARTIST:
Eanger Irving Couse (1866-1936) (Pronounced like "house") American Portrait Painter

Eanger Couse was born and raised on a Michigan farm. As a boy he began drawing people of the Chippewa tribe who lived near the farm. He studied at the Art Institute of Chicago. When Couse moved to New Mexico, he painted the Pueblo people living near Taos. Many artists and writers moved to the northern New Mexico area in the early 1900's. This area was still unsettled. Settlers had flooded into other areas because of the national expansion idea called Manifest Destiny.

MAKE AN OBSERVATION DRAWING! Paint a piece of fruit on rough and smooth types of paper that you have on hand like paper bags, copy paper etc.

THE TIMES:
Manifest Destiny was a general notion that people of the nation shared. They believed that it was the destiny of the United States to expand westward past the Louisiana Territory all the way to the west coast. It was not an actual policy, but the Democrat party used it in the 1840's to justify the War with Mexico. Americans won the war and acquired the territory that now includes the states of Texas, New Mexico, Arizona, Nevada, Utah, and parts of Colorado and Wyoming for a payment of $15 million. Mexicans living in these territories had a choice to leave or become American citizens with full rights and privileges. People of this time felt that the purpose of expansion was to bring democracy to all people and that other countries would not use the land for democratic purposes.

Papers have different qualities which affect the values of the colors. One quality to be aware of is paper texture, also called tooth. When the pencil goes over a rough texture it leaves white spaces in the grooves, which makes a lighter value on the paper.

This apple was drawn on bond paper, which has a very smooth surface. It is so slick that it is difficult to blend one color over another.

The charcoal paper used for this apple has a slight texture. The white of the paper shows through. With plenty of tooth, colors can be layered on top of each other. Here blue easily layers over red.

Very rough paper creates lighter values since color does not reach the deep grooves. This leaves more of the paper showing between the colored areas.

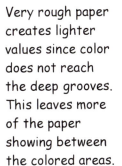

When water is applied to the textured paper on the left, the white areas are filled in. The effect is dramatic, Colors appear brighter and the values appear darker as shown here.

Lesson 3

How to Tint and Shade

Techniques

To tint a color the color pencil is used with less pressure. This allows more of the white paper to show, resulting in a tint.

When using watercolor pencils, the more water you add to the pencil marks, the lighter the value will become. You spread the pigment over a broader area of white paper.

To shade a color you can guess that layering black over the color will do the trick. This will make the color darker, but may not always be the color you desire. Another option for shading is to use a color that is darker than the original color. Here a green leaf is shaded with red. A yellow pot is shaded with red. A yellow box is shaded with blue. A red dragon is shaded with blue.

SOMETHING TO TRY: Draw a simple object of one color from real life. Set it up near a window or other light source so that you can see light and dark areas. Draw the object and fill it in with its color. Use less pressure to create tints. Shade the color using a darker color pencil.

Paint a scene that shows light and shadow. Select a photograph that clearly shows light and shaded areas. Press lightly on the pencil to create tinted areas with the watercolor pencils. Press harder or mix with darker colors to create shaded areas within the painting. Use techniques shown on the previous page.

Final Project
Lesson 4

Application

Student Gallery

Student work by Lavender Huskey shows tinting on the topside of the rock. Shaded areas are seen on the side of the rock. Tinted and shaded areas are also seen in the forest greenery.

YOU WILL NEED

- watercolor pencils
- watercolor brush
- watercolor paper
- water container
- masking tape
- paper towels

THE SUBJECT

Find a picture or photograph where the sunlight hits some part of the objects. Look for tinted areas and shaded areas.

LOOK BACK! Did you select a photograph that showed tinted and shaded areas? Did you use tinting and shading in your work of art?

Lesson 1

unit 6
neutral colors

Student work by Stephen B. uses neutral colors.

Vocabulary and Creative Exercise

When mixing colors that are opposite each other on the color wheel, they become neutral colors. Neutral colors look brown or gray.

using creativity

Creativity happens when we change things in our experience. We can become aware of things that were always there, but that we previously missed. In this exercise you will become more aware by listening instead of looking.

TRY IT: Listening makes you more aware of what's in the world. Dress comfortably. Find an outdoor spot to relax. Experience the world around you through sight and sound. Close your eyes for a minute before you begin to draw. The world sounds different in the fall and winter than it does during summer months. This is especially true after a snowfall or during a windy fall day when dry leaves crackle and shift in the wind. Open your eyes. Draw a picture from your experience with the sounds of the season. You will still be drawing what you see, but you will see more, see new, or see differently because of what you heard.

OBJECTIVE: to hear the world and to use the experience as inspiration for artwork.

Look at Neutral Color in Art   Lesson 2

Art Appreciation

Imagine being given the job of cutting down a large tree with only one small ax. The tool would not be big enough for the task. Imagine being given the job of drawing a tree in color with only one brown pencil. Again the tool is not big enough for the task. We can do it, but the results will be boring. We need a larger selection of browns. By mixing any primary color with the secondary color opposite it on the color wheel, you can make a new brown. We call these colors neutral colors. They vary from grays to browns, depending on which colors are used in the mixture. Notice the variety of neutrals found in this painting of a Connecticut Senator.

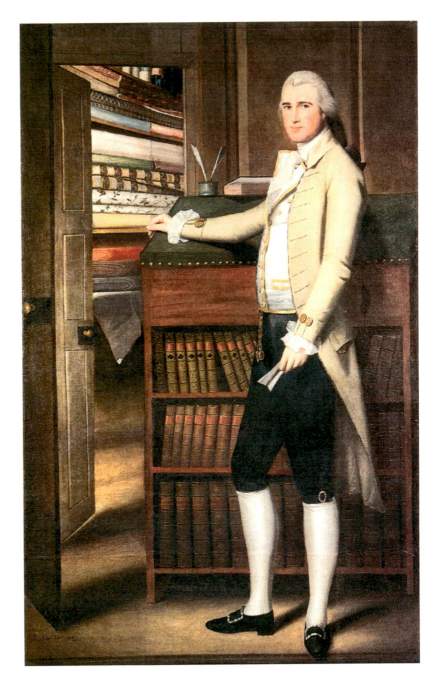

Ralph Earl (1751-1801) Elijah Boardman. 1789.
Photo Credit: Dover Publications Inc.

Gray: dark gray is seen in the desk top, ink jar, and some of the fabrics in the background.

Yellow-brown: the floor, wooden walls, door, and book covers show tints of yellow.

Reddish-brown: the wood of the desk is much redder than the wood around it.

33

Art History

THE ARTIST
Ralph Earl (1751-1801)
American Traveling Painter

Ralph Earl, like so many of the colonial craftsmen, was self-taught. He worked as an itinerant painter, one that traveled from town to town. In 1775, Earl visited Lexington and Concord, which were the sites of recent battles in the American Revolution, and made engravings of the battle scenes. The prints were pro-revolutionary even though Earl later decided to remain a Loyalist and eventually escaped to Europe. Untrained artists, like Earl, were plentiful in the early part of our nation as they traveled throughout the colonies to make a living.

THE TIMES:

From Colonial America to the mid-1840's traveling painters could make a living by following the American pioneers. These traveling artists went to where Americans were settling. They made art without having gone to an official school to learn the trade. They painted portraits of businessmen and their families who created towns, homes, and settlements. During this time there were few places to stay for the night. Traveling artists would be welcomed into the homes of their customers. They ate with them, and brought news of what was happening in other parts of the growing nation.

MAKE AN OBSERVATION PAINTING!

You can work from a photograph found in a magazine, book, or other printed material. You can draw dark marks like the stripes on this cat. The neutral gray area did not need to be drawn in. When the wet brush was washed over the stripes, the paint was pulled into the white area as well, making it light gray. Try mixing two colors to get gray.

Lesson 3

How to Mix Browns and Neutral Colors

Techniques

To make colors less bright, mix colors across from each other on the color wheel. When this happens colors turn brown or gray. These are called neutral colors.

Shown above are the rich varieties of browns you have available in a twelve pencil set. From left to right is golden brown by itself, copper beech (dark brown) by itself, a mixture of deep cadmium (yellow) and imperial purple, a mixture of orange chrome and spectrum blue, a mixture of deep vermilion and grass green, and a mixture of crimson lake and mineral green.

SOMETHING TO TRY: Make some squares on a piece of watercolor paper. Mix the colors in your set that are opposite each other on the color wheel. Blend with water to see the intensity of the mixtures. If you have grays or browns in your color pencil set apply them to the paper also. Keep the color chart as a reference so that your remember how to make a wide range of neutral colors for future paintings.

Final Project Lesson 4

Application

Choose a favorite animal for the subject and make a watercolor pencil painting. Instead of using a brown color pencil where you see brown, mix the neutral color using orange over blue, red over green, or violet over yellow. Refer to the color chart you made from the previous page.

Student Gallery

Student work by Connor Piil shows a wonderful variety of mixed neutral colors.

YOU WILL NEED

- watercolor pencils
- watercolor brush
- watercolor paper
- water container
- masking tape
- paper towels

THE SUBJECT

Animals are a favorite subject for many students. Drawing from real life is a great way to study the colors of the animal. If real animals aren't available, use photographs.

LOOK BACK! Did you show neutral colors by overlapping colors that are opposite each other on the color wheel, then blending with water and brush?

The Elements Combined: Soft and Hard Edges

This additional lesson shows how to create a dynamic painting as color is filled in right up against other colors. With hard edges, one color abruptly stops as another begins. Soft edges gradually blend into another color or into the white of the paper. These techniques can be used with any subject. Choose your own subject and follow the steps on this page.

Set up a group of two or three objects in front of you. Draw them on watercolor paper with pencil. Erase as needed. Fill in the spaces with the watercolor pencils. Place the color up to the edges.

Control the edges with the paint brush. Here the paint brush is used right up against the edge of the shoe, creating a hard edge. Add water where you want to fade out a color like on this table top, to make a soft edge.

Add water to each color space for a hard edge. Allow one edge to dry completely before painting an edge that adjoins it.

The finished painting has clear hard edges within the shoe design and soft edges on the surface of the table.

Lesson 1

values of colors unit 7

Vocabulary and Creative Exercise

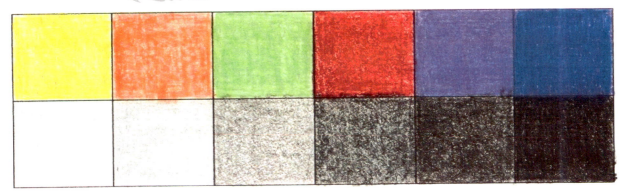

Colors have value. Compare the colors, yellow, orange, green, red, purple, and blue to the grays on the value scale.

Student work by Lavender Huskey shows yellow coming forward and darker colors sitting back in the picture space. All light colors seem to move forward in the picture space when surrounded by dark colors.

using creativity

Artists tend to use intuition or their own gut feeling when making decisions about their art. It may be hard to decide what value a color is at first. With practice you will get better at matching values. Try this fun exercise which will have you make a lot of decisions about the values of colors.

TRY IT: Find a color photograph of a face. It could be of an animal or a person. Make sure the photograph is large enough to see clearly. It should be about 6"-9" high. Cut the photo in half vertically. Glue one half of the photo onto a sheet of drawing paper. Using a drawing pencil, draw the other half. You will be drawing a mirror image to create a whole face. While drawing with a graphite pencil only, match the values to the color values in the photograph.

OBJECTIVE: See colors and match the values of those colors to a gray scale.

Look at Color Values in Art   Lesson 2

What colors do you see in the white dress? Is the value of the blue shadow in the dress the same as the value in some areas of the sky? Look at the value of the water. That value is repeated in the upper left corner of the sky. Similar values in colors help our eye travel from one area to the next.

Frank Benson, *Sunlight*, 1909.
Photo Credit: Dover Publications Inc.

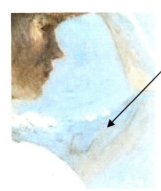

The value of the shaded area of the white sleeve is similar to the value of the sky.
The grass has values of light, middle, and dark.

Art Appreciation

THE ARTIST:

Frank Benson (1862-1951)
American Impressionist Painter

Frank Benson was from Salem, Massachusetts and lived there most of his life. He taught at the Boston Museum School and painted in Maine during the summer months. He painted many pictures of his family playing in the grasses along the Maine coastline. Benson became famous in the United States and Paris for his Impressionistic paintings of his wife and daughters. Benson had an interest in hunting and fishing and later in life he made etchings of wildlife. He had a successful life as an artist and instructor.

MAKE AN IMAGINATION DRAWING!

Draw onto a colored piece of paper using color pencils. No water will be added. The colors will appear different on colored paper than on white paper. Do not worry too much about getting the colors just right. Just look at the color combinations and choose to use color in the way that you like. Choose any subject. Play around.

THE TIMES:

American Impressionism started when the work of French Impressionist painters was displayed in the 1880's in Boston and New York. They were so impressed by the way light and bright colors were used that they took up a similar way of painting. Impressionism had developed as a loose style of painting twenty years earlier in Paris. It caught on in America and was widely accepted by the public. Artists' colonies developed around the ideas of Impressionism. In the colonies artists could work and be around other artists with the same interests. They flourished in areas where the scenery was beautiful, living was cheap, and which had large cities nearby where artists could promote their work. American Impressionism was widely followed for forty years, until 1913 when the Amory Show brought new and more daring art from Europe to the American eye. Professional artists had always looked to Europe for their training. Nearly every notable artist, including Frank Benson, spent some time in Europe. They picked up the technical training there and then they would often come back to America to make art with American themes. The Armory show was the final great influence of Europe on American art. After 1913 American artists took hold of the ideas they saw presented there and pushed the boundaries of art in their own unique ways. The new leaders in art would come from New York, not from Paris, France.

Lesson 3

How to Add Color Values in a Still-Life

Techniques

A drawing can be no better than the arrangement of the objects. Follow these tips on arranging and adding value to make an interesting still life.

When **arranging** a still life, follow these tips:
- Choose objects with a variety of shapes and colors.
- Notice surfaces and backgrounds and add colorful cloths as part of the set up.
- Overlap the objects.
- Look for strong colors and draw each object in its color or in a light color like yellow.

When **drawing** a still life, avoid finishing one object before going on to the next. Colors relate. Let all the colors within a picture develop together. Develop one object to a certain point, then give the rest of the drawing the same treatment.
- Make a line drawing first. Make corrections as you draw.
- Add middle values throughout the painting. Add darker values and finally add details.

SOMETHING TO TRY: Arrange a variety of objects into a group, following the instructions for arranging a still life. Draw the still life. Focus on developing all the objects throughout the picture as described above.

Set up a still life using real objects from around the house. Place the light source on one side so that you can see light and dark areas on the objects. Tape the paper to a board. Fill in with color, and then add water to create a painting.

Final Project Lesson 4

Application

Student Gallery

YOU WILL NEED

- watercolor pencils
- watercolor brush
- watercolor paper
- water container
- masking tape
- paper towels

THE SUBJECT

Choose small items to put together in a still-life set up. Place on the table in front of you, just above your painting materials. Choose fruits, vegetables, plants, flower arrangements, or gather grasses from the backyard and put into a display.

Student work by Lavender Huskey shows attention to shading the objects and the shadows on the table. Light and dark leaves show contrast in values.

LOOK BACK! Did you use different values in the picture? Which two values show contrast within your work?

42

COMPOSITION

Do you challenge yourself by drawing subjects that are new for you or are slightly unfamiliar? When a subject is unfamiliar, it helps to draw it repeatedly. We know from experience that the more it is drawn, the better the artist becomes at drawing it. When artists draw a scene, they know that the first attempt will not be their best. So they often make quick sketches. They draw and redraw. They then rearrange the parts of the scene, knowing that each new solution is better than the last. Arranging the parts is called composition. You can study ways to make good compositions as you work with the following ideas: direction and movement, rhythm, and point of view including front, back, high, and low. You will also learn some measurement and proportion techniques as you draw buildings, the figure, faces, and interiors. We think you will enjoy drawing these new subjects. Remember to have fun and choose objects that you like!

Front View and Side View
by C.G.

Lesson 1

unit 8
direction and movement

Vocabulary and Creative Exercise

You know that line helps us outline a shape. It can also be used to create texture. In this unit we will see how line can be used in compositions to suggest direction and movement.

Horizontal lines communicate stability or calm.

Vertical lines suggest strength, dominance, or authority.

Diagonal lines suggest movement. We can see the diagonal angle of the girls' bodies and this helps to show that they are moving forward.

using creativity

A picture starts with an idea. The idea can begin with a scene, an event, a change in the weather, a memory, a mood, or anything else that stirs up a response in you. When people are a part of your artwork, it is best to use real people to look at. Drawing on the spot teaches you to draw quickly and to remember what you saw once the people have changed positions. With practice you'll be able to capture a scene quickly and accurately. Don't be shy about drawing in public. You could draw at rodeos, ballgames, a circus, parades, fairs, talent shows, plays, or trade shows. The people who notice you and respond to your activity will usually be positive in their comments.

TRY IT: Draw your observations of people doing an activity that interests you. What are people doing around you today? Draw from directly observing a scene.

OBJECTIVE: to draw from observation of real figures, increasing skills in figure drawing.

Look at Direction and Movement in Art   Lesson 2

You know how to make an object move in real space, but how do you show a moving object on the space of a flat piece of paper? Movement usually involves diagonal lines. Look at how Thomas Eakins uses diagonal lines in the oars and the bent positions of the bodies.

Thomas Eakins, *The Biglin Brothers Racing*, 1873-74.
Photo Credit: Dover Publications Inc.

There are no vertical lines in this painting. This painting has many horizontal lines.

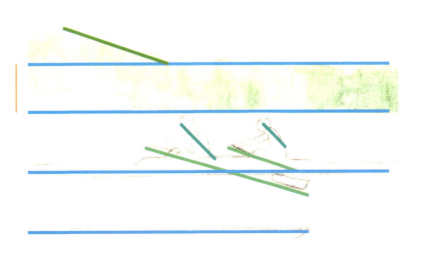

The blue-green diagonal lines are angled more sharply than the green diagonal lines.

Art Appreciation

45

Art History

THE ARTIST:
Thomas Eakins (1844-1916)
American Realist Painter

Eakins chose to paint scenes around the home of his friends and family with accurate realism. He was one of the first artists after the Civil War to use photography for his sketches. This gave his paintings a very realistic appearance. "Realism has always been important in American art. Americans loved American life as it was lived, and they wanted to read about it in their books (Tom Sawyer by Mark Twain) and see it in their art" (Batterberry 86). Eakins was best known for giving us a picture of true American life.

MAKE AN OSERVATION PICTURE!
How do we live today? Sports are still a huge pastime for Americans. Draw a picture of people participating in an athletic activity like Thomas Eakins did in *The Biglin Brothers Racing*. You may want to use a photograph as a reference or if you are familiar with the sport, draw from your memory. Lightly sketch the figures first, making adjustments as needed, then finish.

THE TIMES:
Nearly one hundred years had passed since America had become a new nation. During that time they had tested the new and original documents governing its citizens. The Constitution, which limited the power of the national government, had resulted in freedoms that men had only imagined before that time. They moved westward, built new communities, new communication systems and were proud of their accomplishments. Many artists felt that there should be a new and unique art as well. They felt that artists did not need to go to Europe for their art education as they had in the past. Thomas Eakins spoke what many American artists were feeling. He said, "If America is to produce great painters, [young art students should] remain in America to peer deeper into the heart of America." Artists began to seek subjects that they found in their own communities. They discovered new ways of painting.

Lesson 3

How to Use Marks to Show Textures

A variety of marks can be made by changing the pressure being used and the patterns of the marks. Below are marks you may want to try putting into your art. Look for the letters that show how some types of marks were used in the picture below.

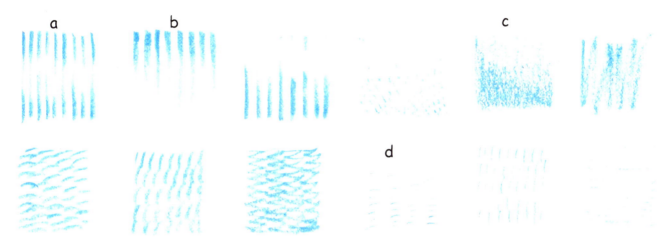

In any subject a variety of lines can be used. There is no one correct way to mark any particular area. The artist chooses what he feels will best describe the surface of what he sees. Here the cupcakes are drawn with parallel lines and lines that cross them. The lines in the table cloth are made by changing the pressure on the pencil from heavy to light as the pencil is lifted from the page at the end of each stroke.

SOMETHING TO TRY: Use colored pencils on drawing paper. Practice different marks using color pencils. Some examples are shown at the top of the page. Choose a few simple subjects, perhaps from the kitchen, and draw from direct observation.

Draw a scene of people in motion. Think about what they are doing, and the direction in which they are heading. Lean the figures into the action or use arms and limbs to show movement.

Student Gallery

Final Project
Lesson 4

Student work by Bert Pace, left, shows movement as the arms and legs of the player are bent to show motion. His body is angled forward. The direction of line in the tackler is even more angled and shows a forward plunge.

Student work by Jared Jenkins, right, shows an upward movement as his arm is raised straight above the head. Both figures are angled in a direction of line that leans toward the basketball hoop. The directions of marks that are shown in the gray background support the upward movement toward the hoop.

YOU WILL NEED

- colored pencil set
- drawing paper
- vinyl eraser

THE SUBJECT

You may want to work from direct observation during the drawing portion of this activity, trying several different positions to show movement. If you are not confident of your ability to show movement by directly observing people, then find a photograph that shows people in motion.

LOOK BACK! Explain what ways movement is shown in your drawing.

The Elements Combined: Shapes and Textures

This additional lesson shows how you might use shapes and textures together in a picture using colored pencils. These techniques can be used with any subject. A furry animal was chosen so that the direction of the lines is clearly seen. A photograph was used as a reference. Choose your own subject and follow the steps on this page using drawing paper.

1. To start, lines and shapes are drawn, erased and redrawn until the form is correct.

2. Texture is added within the shapes. Lines to show fur are drawn in the direction of the fur.

3. Red and ochre pencils are used throughout the head and body.

4. Ochre pencil is drawn over the red lines. Dark brown is added.

5. This finished work shows the texture of the bunny fur. Many shapes are no longer clear, but hidden by the fur.

Lesson 1

Vocabulary and Creative Exercise

The elements of art are space, line, shape, texture, value, form, and color. Rhythm is created when we repeat any of these elements on the space of the page. Here the leaf shape and green color of the leaf creates rhythm across the page.

using creativity

One uses both their eyes and their mind when drawing from direct observation. Our eyes see, but our mind tells us what we see. Sometimes we rely more on our mind than on our sight. People tend to walk through the world with an invisible wall about ten feet in front of them. They rarely take notice of what is beyond that point. Train yourself to see into the distance. Start really looking with the simple exercise described below. Your world becomes bigger as you take notice of more within it.

TRY IT: Step outdoors and focus on a part of your hand for about 5 seconds. Then look into the distance and pick out an object, focusing on it for 5 seconds. Look back at your hand for 5 more seconds then switch to the distant object for another 5 seconds. Do this for at least three minutes, switching your focus from near to far. When this exercise is practiced often, you begin to see more accurately.
Draw a picture of a scene in the distance. Focus on the distant scene, and then switch focus to the paper to draw.

OBJECTIVE: to exercise the eye and the mind to see more of the world by changing focus from near to far, to gain the habit of looking at the subject in 5 second intervals while drawing.

50

Look at Rhythm in Art   Lesson 2

Imagine walking on a path through a picture. If the path went only half way, we would miss looking at the entire picture. That's why artists make paths through the entire picture. Artists use rhythm by creating lines, colors, or shapes to create a path that our eyes follow. In this painting by Winslow Homer a path is created from side to side by the boys' figures. They even hold hands to make a connection.

Winslow Homer, *Snap the Whip*, 1872.
Photo Credit: Dover Publications Inc.

These figures create a rhythm that carries our eyes from right to left and back.

THE ARTIST: Winslow Homer (1836-1910)
American Realist Painter

Winslow Homer spent his boyhood out of doors, giving him a love for the country. He worked for a lithographer and received art training. At the outbreak of the Civil War, he went south with the Union forces. He sent back many illustrations to *Harper's Weekly*, the magazine he was employed at. He painted pictures of the war, which brought him attention from Americans and Europeans. He was an adventurous man and traveled, using those things he saw as subject matter for his paintings. As an adult, he painted many pictures of country life. Many include children in activities of playing games, at school, and picking berries.

MAKE AN IMAGINATION DRAWING! What do you do with your friends? Draw a group of figures that are involved in a single activity. The group might be playing a game as in Homer's *Snap the Whip* or involved in an activity at the playground.

THE TIMES:

People who are captured and sold and who then work for their owner without pay are called slaves. They are owned in much the same way a farmer might own an ox and expect it to work for him. Even before America had become a nation, slaves were regularly shipped from Africa. Slavery became a part of the structure of the new country. As the new nation began to grow, the northern states began to depend on new machines and worked in factories and on small farms. They had less need for slaves. The southern states developed large plantations, growing crops of cotton and tobacco. They needed even more slaves to work in the fields. Many people felt that slavery was wrong and spoke against owning people. But others said what they did was right because they believed that people whose skin color was different from their own were inferior. In 1858, while running for President, Abraham Lincoln said that the country could not permanently be "half slave and half free". Slave owners from the South said that every state had a right to make its own laws and to choose whether slaves would be free or not. These strong differences in opinion led to the Civil War. Winslow Homer was twenty-five when the war started and drew both the miseries endured by soldiers and their heroism and spirit. Photography was developed during this time so many portraits of soldiers and generals were made as they waited in camps before the battles began. Photography was not fast enough to capture moving objects so scenes of battles had to be created by artists like Homer. Slavery was abolished in the entire nation once the brutal war ended.

Art History

Lesson 3
How to Use Colored Pencils - Dry

ERASING: It is difficult to erase color pencils. An area can be lightened (as shown in the first example) so that another color can be applied over the area (as shown in the second example). Use a white vinyl eraser with color pencils.

THE PROBLEM WITH A HEAVY-HANDED APPROACH: Paper catches color in its rough surface. Pressing hard, as shown in the light green area, fills up the surface, making it slick so that other colors cannot be layered over it.

THE BENEFITS OF A LIGHT-HANDED APPROACH: When color is applied with lighter pressure white areas of the paper are left for the dark green and yellow to connect to. In this way one color can be layered over another.

Step 1. Draw the outline of the object. Use a graphite pencil, which can be erased easily. Use drawing paper.

Step 2. The red, yellow, and orange lines of the leaf are drawn first so that green can be added around the distinctive lines.

Step 3. Draw light green areas between the yellow-orange lines with even, light pressure.

Step 4. Layer dark green over the light green at the edges.

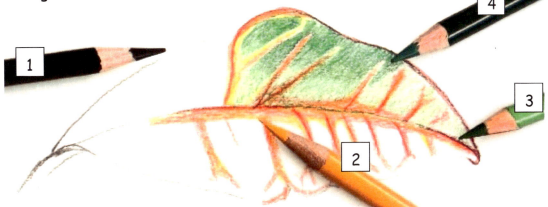

SOMETHING TO TRY: Work with color blending using a simple object.

Final Project Lesson 4

Application

Using your imagination, draw a favorite subject in a scene that shows rhythm. Obtain rhythm in several ways:

Repeat the main object itself, as in a herd of buffalo rather than just one buffalo.

Repeat a minor object, not the main one, as in a car with a background of many trees, repeating the lines of the tree trunks.

Repeat a specific color throughout the picture.

Student Gallery

Student work above is by Olga L. B.

YOU WILL NEED

- colored pencil set
- drawing paper
- vinyl eraser

THE SUBJECT

Draw from observation. Show the subject using rhythm. The subject can be:
- machines
- people
- animals
- plants

LOOK BACK! What element or object in the picture is repeated? Draw an imaginary path with your finger to show the direction of rhythm.

The Elements Combined: Blending Colors

This additional lesson shows how to blend using colored pencils on drawing paper. Drawing paper is the perfect surface for colored pencil techniques. These techniques can be used with any subject. Choose your own subject and follow the step on this page.

Draw the basic shapes on the page with a light colored pencil such as yellow or ochre. Then fill in the colors creating solid light areas. Apply little pressure as you fill in small areas at a time. Move the pencil back and forth, as you slowly pull it toward you. Take care to stop at the edges of the shape.

Go over each area again, using the same color of a darker value. Or you can use the same color but use more pressure to create dark values. Start at the darkest edge of the object and as you move the pencil toward the opposite edge, lift up gradually, allowing the color to blend into the first layer. The blending in the white areas was done with blue pencil first and overlapped with gray.

Lesson 1

unit 10
front and back points of view

Vocabulary and Creative Exercise

Point of view is what you see from where you stand. A side view is not always the most interesting position from which to view an object. The picture at the left is what the viewer above would see from the front. The picture at the right is what the viewer above would see from the back.

using creativity

Drawings and paintings should begin to express who you are as a person. Your experiences are your own and the subjects you choose to draw are unique to you. Even though others may draw the same subject, it will be different from your view. As you continue to make art, choose subjects that you like.

TRY IT: Choose a subject that you like and can study from the front and the back. Draw a front view and then a back view.

> OBJECTIVE: to develop awareness of personal expression within defined limits of using point of view.

56

Look at Front and Back Points of View in Art   Lesson 2

Art Appreciation

We are familiar with seeing figures in motion today because we have cameras and video equipment that capture those images. But in the nineteenth century artists had to study figures very carefully, usually while real people were posing for the painting. It was probably not easy to keep the boat still while the artist painted the figures in this painting called, *The Boating Party*. These figures show a woman from a front view, a child from the front view, and a man from a back view. Set against a brilliant blue background and the lush yellow curve of the boat, this painting emphasizes the figures.

Mary Cassatt (1844-1926) *The Boating Party*. 1893-94.
Photo Credit: Dover Publications Inc.

In a front point of view (woman), features such as the eyes, nose, and mouth are in full view. In a back point of view (man), these features cannot be seen unless the face is tilted into a partial side view.

THE ARTIST:
Mary Cassatt (1844-1926)
American Impressionist Painter

Mary Cassatt was recognized as a master artist during her lifetime. Born in America, her family moved to Europe for a time, then back to America. Cassatt studied art at the Pennsylvania Academy of Fine Arts, the oldest art school in America. As an adult, she bravely decided to leave her family and to study art in Europe at a time when women did not travel without male companionship. She became a friend to artists in France within a group called Impressionists. She painted scenes of mothers and children in daily activities and gave us a view into what women did in that period. Sewing and caring for children were some of her themes. One of the most valuable contributions she made to America was to encourage wealthy American patrons to purchase Impressionist work. In this way she was helping her friends sell their work and because of her we have many Impressionist works within our American art museums.

MAKE AN OBSERVATION DRAWING! Compile a list of activities that require the figure to bend such as running, hopping, swinging, kneeling, or dancing. Have someone act these things out for you as you draw what you see. These may be very quick sketches.

THE TIMES:

When Mary was a teenager the United States of America began work on a transcontinental railroad, one that would stretch all the way across the continent. At this time huge numbers of bison still roamed free throughout the American West. No one had yet heard of a telephone. Gas lamps still lit the streets of cities in the East. At the age of 22 she traveled to Paris France, known as "the City of Light" because of its many gas lamps, beautiful new buildings, and outdoor cafés. Paris had been rebuilt in order to help people forget the awful results of the French Revolution and turmoil of its recent past. Mary had come to study the old European master works, but to her delight French painters were not copying the past. They boldly painted in an entirely new way. Bright, fresh new colors were applied in loose strokes. Their way of painting was more immediate too. Instead of carefully planning out compositions and making a dark underpainting*, many Impressionists applied paint in dabs, lines, and thick layers. They started with white cloth canvas. They worked outdoors instead of indoors. Mary had arrived in Europe just in time to meet the Impressionists!

*Underpainting is a method used since the 1300's in which the arrangement and figures were painted onto the surface and the values of dark to light painted in detail. Color was then applied in layers over the underpainting in glazes or thin washes.

Art History

Lesson 3
How to Make a Full Color Drawing

Techniques

When choosing a place to begin a drawing, start with the main object, like the horse. Once the object is drawn on the page in the right place, draw what is around that object. When adding color, work on the object and then skip to the colors in the background to see how the colors look when sitting next to each other. Go back and forth from object to background.

Begin full color drawings by placing outlines within the space of the page. Change lines as needed by erasing and redrawing. Notice that the lines are not all the same thickness or value. Shaded areas have darker lines.

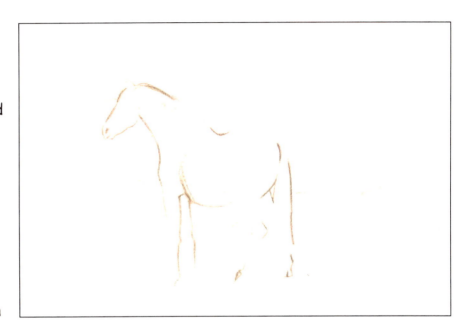

Place colors in certain areas, without bringing them to a finished point. The horse is not finished before putting in the green trees or blue sky. Small areas are colored all over the picture. Continue to work this way until the space has as much color as desired.

SOMETHING TO TRY:
Make a full color drawing as explained above. Vary the lines. Color the entire picture space before finishing any one area so that you can see color relationships.

Draw a subject from a photograph. Make sure the photograph is sharply focused, not blurry or containing special effects. Choose a photograph with a front or back point of view and bright colors.

Final Project
Lesson 4

Application

Student Gallery

Student work by Holly Heckman shows a group of horses. The white horse stands out. The entire background is filled with color. She has clearly emphasized the white horse in a front point of view.

YOU WILL NEED

- colored pencil set
- sketch paper
- vinyl eraser

THE SUBJECT

Choose a subject from a photograph. The photograph should have these characteristics:
- Bold colors
- Show a front or back point of view
- Include a background

LOOK BACK! Did you show a front or back point of view? Did you fill in the background and the main objects with color?

Lesson 1

high and low points of view
unit 1.1

Vocabulary and Creative Exercise

Changing the point from which you view the object gives very different results. A high point of view allows you look down upon the object while a low point of view allows one to see under the object.

 VIEWED HIGH ABOVE THE OBJECT

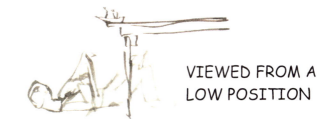 VIEWED FROM A LOW POSITION

using creativity

Some people draw dark, heavy lines. Some people draw light, wispy lines. Others draw in short strokes, in long strokes, or dots and dashes. All methods are good, but the creative person does not stick to only one approach. It takes courage to try something new since one gets comfortable with the familiar. To be creative, one needs to attempt new ways of drawing.

TRY IT: First evaluate how you tend to use lines. Decide on a different approach to use. Draw a simple object similar to the pitcher shown above. Concentrate on a way of drawing the lines and textures that might better express what you see.

OBJECTIVE: to develop direct observation skills, eye-hand coordination, and the ability to break from a single approach to drawing by choosing line that best describes what is seen.

Look at High and Low Points of View in Art   Lesson 2

This high point of view allows the viewer to see the city street below the train. We see the top side of the train. We also see the city in the distance. Land takes up more picture space than sky.

John Sloan, (1871-1951) *The City from Greenwich Village*, 1922.
Photo Credit: Dover Publications Inc.

This low point of view is of the same train, but at a different time of day and different view point. We now see the underside of the train. Heads are at the bottom of the picture, level with the viewer's eyesight. Sky takes up more picture space in this work.

John Sloan, (1871-1951) *Six O' Clock*.
C. 1912
Photo Credit: Dover Publications Inc.

In a high view point (shown in the top painting) the viewer is high and looks down to see mostly ground. The artist sets himself above the action. The subway train angles downward to the lower right of the painting. In a low viewpoint (shown in the lower painting) the viewer is low and looks up to the elevated train. The viewer sees much sky. The train's angle goes up toward the top right of the painting.

THE ARTIST:
John Sloan (1871-1951)
American Realist Painter and Political Cartoonist

John Sloan studied art in Philadelphia then gained employment there by making full-page color illustrations for news stories. He also made illustrations for magazines. Much of his work was political commentary. That means he made cartoons about what was going on in the nation's politics. In 1902 he moved to New York and became a part of the Ashcan school, a group of artists who painted pictures of everyday urban life. Sloan's painting was thought to be political as well as his cartoons. He painted the poorer working class in their activities at home and on the job. In 1910 Sloan joined the Socialist Party in America. He said in his autobiography, Gist of Art (1939), "Ever since the Great War broke out in 1914 this world has been a crazy place to live in. I hate war and I put the hatred into cartoons in the Masses. I had great hopes for the world's socialist parties until 1914. Then I saw how they fell apart. Some of the leaders were killed; the emotional patterns of national pride set one country against another. I became disillusioned." He left the party and years later became concerned for the native people living in New Mexico. He lived there for part of each year and painted the land and the people of New Mexico.

THE TIMES:

The American Socialist Party began in 1901. Some thought it was the way to help the poor achieve equality with those that were wealthier. The idea flourished in urban areas where poor and wealthy lived in close contact and among some Immigrant populations. It did not last long as a strong political movement. World War I broke out in 1914 and the bloodshed caused by Socialist governments in other parts of the world convinced many that this path of government control was not the answer that they'd been looking for. The world still struggles with the ideas of socialism, where government authorities control income levels, job availability, food supplies, and more. In America today people either believe that the government should control all areas of life or that it should be limited in its power to do so. Capitalism allows individuals to make more choices. When people choose how to educate their children, choose to change jobs as they like, or choose what kind of foods and supplies to purchase, they allow capitalism to work.

MAKE A MEMORY DRAWING! Draw a scene from your neighborhood just like John Sloan did. He was always looking at the people around him. He liked to put those things into his paintings.

Lesson 3
How to Draw an Ellipse

An ellipse is a circle seen at an angle. There are many circles in art so it is important to learn to draw an ellipse at different angles. Ellipses show up in cups, on hats, or any cylindrical form. At eye level the ellipse seems closed. Above and below the ellipse, it seems more open until it looks like a circle.

If a glass is positioned so that you can see a wide ellipse at the top, then the bottom will show the same.

⟵ Yes! – No! ⟶

Ellipse ends are round, never pointed.

MAKE AN OBSERVATION DRAWING!
Draw a round object from a high view point. As you draw make sure that all the ellipses are at a similar tilt.

Hannah Gibson observed this cowboy hat from a high view point.

Techniques

Final Project Lesson 4

Application

Look for high or low viewpoints in real-life objects. High angles often give us a better picture of small flat creatures like the frog below. Sometimes you will have to arrange objects to get these types of special view points. You could place the object onto the floor of a low table and look down upon it from a seated position. Draw the object you've chosen and what is around the object to fill the page with color.

Student Gallery

Student work is by Hannah Gibson. She worked from a photograph and shows a low point of view.

The picture is by student, Timothy Ichiyasu. He looks down upon a frog from a high view point.

YOU WILL NEED

- colored pencil set
- sketch paper
- vinyl eraser

THE SUBJECT

A picture can be composed from any objects around your home. Large plastic reptile figures may make good subjects when looking from above. Find ways to place objects above or below so that you can work with high or low points of view.

LOOK BACK! Did you choose to sit above or below the subject? Did you make a work of art that shows it from a high or low point of view?

Lesson 1

Emphasis of Details
unit 12

Vocabulary and Creative Exercise

The artist can arrange the subject so that special details or features that identify the subject are more clearly shown. The artist, J. Audubon, in this picture of a Red-shouldered Hawk, positions the top bird so that we can see the markings on the back, while the lower bird is positioned so that we see the details on the stomach and underside of the tail. In this way detailed markings are emphasized.

Photo Credit: Dover Publications Inc. NY.

using creativity

Artists are like explorers. They have only a vague idea of where they are headed because they travel to new places. These are places others have not been before so there is no map or technique to follow. They keep their eyes open for new discoveries along the way.

TRY IT: Take a walk. Discover something new in the natural world. Let your eyes and your mind wander from one object to the next object. Soon your mind will make connections which will inspire a new work of art. Draw your observations. Give attention to details. Think about how to arrange the object so that the most important details are shown.

OBJECTIVE: to activate a response that stems from observations of the real world.

Look at Emphasis in Art   Lesson 2

The white Orchid stands out because of the dark background that surrounds it. The hummingbirds stand out because they are dark against the foggy light background. These changes in value give emphasis to the main objects of the painting. There is a more subtle way to emphasize specific points in a painting. Look at the two hummingbirds in the background. The artist has chosen to position the birds so that one shows the back of the bird, while the other shows the belly of the birds. In this way we get more information about the special features of the bird.

Martin Johnson Heade (1819-1904) *Two Hummingbirds Above a White Orchid,* 1870's Oil on Canvas. 18 ½ x 10 1/8th in. Photo Credit: Dover Publications Inc., NY.

Back of Hummingbird

Front Belly and Neck of Hummingbird

THE ARTIST:

Martin Johnson Heade (1819-1904) Landscape artist known for tropical birds and flowers

Martin Johnson Heade was born in Pennsylvania. His father was a storekeeper running a general store and post office in Lumberville. Heade received his first art training from Edward Hicks, a well known folk artist living in the nearby town of Newton. You can see the work of Hicks in Artistic Pursuits Elementary Book One, Unit 9. The realism in Heade's works was influenced by other painters of the time known as the Romantics. Smooth even layers of paint, misty scenes, and exact representations of leaves, flowers, and other objects are a mark of that group. Heade made friendships with artists of the Hudson River School where he became interested in landscapes. These artists sometimes traveled abroad and their paintings influenced Heade. Inspired by travel, he went to Brazil in his mid-40's where he painted many small works of hummingbirds. These paintings were intended to be used in a book titled "The Gems of Brazil", but the book was never published. Heade made two more trips to the tropics within that decade. For the rest of his life he painted lush foliage in still-lifes and tropical birds found in the state of Florida. To a person who is not from Florida, the one area of the US where tropical plants grow, Heade's work can seem a bit foreign.

THE TIMES:

Movements in art are usually a reaction against another movement or idea. Movements influence how artists paint and the subjects they choose to paint. The Romantic Movement, which began in Europe, was popular among people in the early 19th century while Heade was growing up. They believed that strong emotion was a good source of inspiration. They often painted emotions such as worry, fear, and honorable accomplishment. While these topics may not have influenced Heade, the manner in which they handled the paint did. Heade's use of dark backgrounds immersed in clouds, fog, or light is found in other Romantic works. Applying the color in smooth layers with even blended tones and precise rendering (drawing) are also marks of the movement. Untamed nature and wilderness areas were common themes of the movement and this is certainly a large part of Heade's work. Artists don't try to paint like others in a movement. However they do go toward things they like and that may attract them to certain groups of artists who have similar ideas. As an artist you make the same types of choices in subjects and manner of painting. Making these choices is the true mark of an artist!

MAKE AN OBSERVATION DRAWING! Place a real or fake flower on a table cloth or other cloth. Draw this view from observing it. Heade made many paintings just like this. His favorite flowers were the Orchids and Magnolias of the South.

Lesson 3
How to Define the Subject

Techniques

Drawings have more power to attract when you give attention to certain details. Focus on the following three details to define your subject.

1. Keep pencils sharp, using a handheld sharpener. Make sharp edges as shown in the bluejay's bill. Sharpen color pencils with care since the "leads" are softer than graphite. The makers of Prismacolor pencils suggest sharpening a graphite pencil in between sharpening color pencils. This will clean off the wax that builds up on the blades of the pencil sharpener.

2. Use hard pressure to make colors darker. Lay down a solid layer of color as shown in the brown and red areas of this bird. The amount of pressure you put on the pencil affects the values in your drawing. To make smooth, even areas of color, keep the pressure on the pencil the same.

3. Overlap one color on top of another. Dark green is drawn over light green, red over yellow, in this hummingbird. Review page 24 where you learned that overlapping colors beside each other on the color wheel makes them appear brighter.

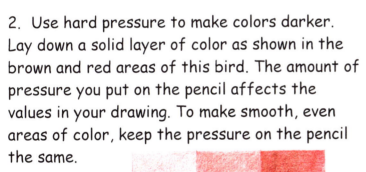

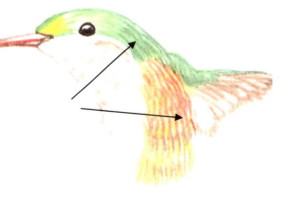

SOMETHING TO TRY: Choose a colorful object to draw, perhaps from a photograph. Draw with color pencils. Remember to keep the pencils sharp. Use pressure for intense color and overlapping colors as shown on this page.

Birds have intricate markings that look beautiful when drawn in colored pencil. Choose a photograph to work from that shows the details of the markings clearly. Show these details in your artwork. Draw the subject in color pencils as you apply the information on the previous page.

Final Project Lesson 4

Application

Student Gallery

YOU WILL NEED

- colored pencil set
- sketch paper
- vinyl eraser

THE SUBJECT

Find a photograph of a bird. Calendar pictures of birds are large enough to see the details clearly. Also look in the library for photographs of birds in the children's section. Choose a bird with markings on the feathers.

LOOK BACK! Did you layer colors, show special markings of the feathers, or use pressure to make colors darker in some areas of your bird painting?

Lesson 1

Vocabulary and Creative Exercise

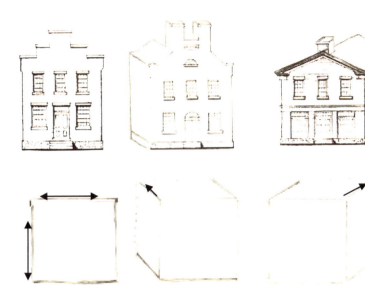

Many buildings are like blocks. From the front we see only horizontal and vertical lines.

From an angle, we see diagonal lines. Notice that the diagonal lines on each block and building go in the same direction at the same angle.

using creativity

When we look at information in a new way we use creativity. Just because we can see the whole object does not mean we must draw it all. Artists learn to pick and choose the information they want in their painting. Robert M. Brown, author of *Writing for a Reader*, states how hesitant most of us are to see things from a different point of view. He says, "We tend to see things only from the point of view that we have been programmed to see them. Like sand crabs, we are afraid to venture very far out of our shells, and if we do go out, we quickly scamper home, backwards." It takes courage not to act like the sand crabs.

TRY IT: Make a pile of something: pencils, books, washcloths, pillows, etc. Imagine you are the size of a sand crab and look into the pile. Draw what you see. Do not show the whole pile, but a section of it. This point of view requires imagination and careful observation of the details.

OBJECTIVE: to increase eye-hand coordination while observing spatial relationships.

Look at Buildings in Art   Lesson 2

The title, *Boomtown*, tells a lot about this picture and the artist's reason for making it. Benton showed the activity of a small town during the industrial age, where vehicles, machines, and industry caused rapid growth to areas throughout the United States in the early 20th century.

Thomas Hart Benton (1889-1975) *Boomtown,* 1928. Oil on Canvas 45 x 54 in.
Photo Credit: Dover Publications Inc.

A cube can be angled to resemble each of the buildings in this painting. Seeing the angles of the lines in a cube simplifies our view of the buildings. In the example at the right, the buildings do not fit perfectly because Benton loved to twist and turn the objects within his pictures. The vertical lines in the buildings on the right are parallel to the right edge of the painting.

THE ARTIST: Thomas Hart Benton (1889-1975) American born, Regionalist painter

Benton painted scenes of Americans in large cities like New York and small farming communities in the Midwest. In his own words, he described his work as "common art for the common man." His popularity with Americans was strongest during the 1930's when he and a few friends started the Regionalist movement. They opposed abstract art and the move toward breaking down social norms through art. His art has a distinctive look as figures, buildings, and clouds curve and swirl in complex compositions. Benton truly had a feel for small town America and put it into his paintings. His studio home is open to the public at the Thomas Hart Benton Home and Studio State Historic Site in Kansas City, Missouri.

MAKE AN OBSERVATION DRAWING
Practice making lines that flow in the direction you observe when drawing blocks. Choose children's blocks, or other cubed objects. Arrange them in different angles and place on a table in front of you. They can be stacked and tilted for interest. Draw the outside edges of the blocks. If you are doing well, pile the blocks in an interesting group and make a more finished drawing.

THE TIMES:

Small towns played an important role in shaping the friendly nature of the American character in the early 20th century. In 1900, most Americans were farmers and small town dwellers. At a time when there was no electricity, their activities followed the sun-rise, beginning work at 4:00 a.m. and continued well after sun-set. There was no running water or indoor bathrooms. In the spring women were seen outdoors washing the family clothing in tubs. Men were seen in the fields walking behind horses attached to small plows. People of small communities had originally gathered for support and safety, and grew to depend on the generosity of their neighbors. They easily welcomed newcomers. People of a town would gather to raise one man's barn or to help build the first general store. Women prepared the meals together and they ate with those that participated in the activity. They had no idea how quickly their lives would change in the next fifty years. Electricity brought lights and new appliances like washers, refrigerators, and cooking stoves. Gasoline powered cars and farm equipment helped farmers haul and work their fields faster. People's needs were met more through the new machines and people needed the help of their neighbor less often. However the good nature which came about through helping each other remained and is often found in many small communities today.

Lesson 3
How to Draw Buildings

Techniques

Look at the way all the horizontal lines line up with the top and bottom of the paper's edge. Look at the way all the vertical lines line up with the left and right sides of the paper's edge. When you draw buildings and other cubed shapes remember to check the edges of the paper and make sure your lines are at the correct angle.

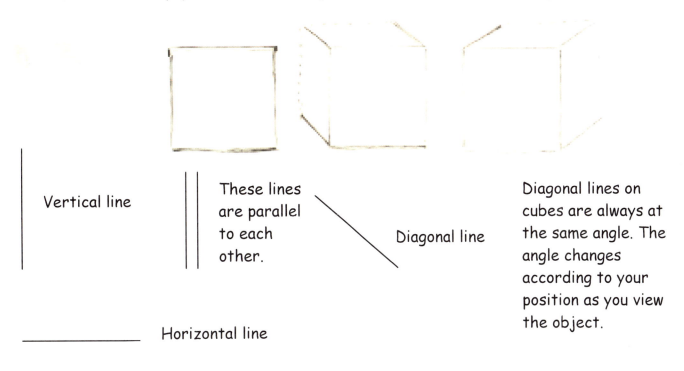

Vertical line

These lines are parallel to each other.

Diagonal line

Diagonal lines on cubes are always at the same angle. The angle changes according to your position as you view the object.

Horizontal line

Windows, doors, and additions to buildings follow the same rules as those for building a cube. Buildings on streets face the same direction so the angles of the lines on each building will remain the same. You can make very straight lines with a ruler. When using a ruler, hold it down firmly with one hand and pull a pencil line along the metal edge with the other hand.

SOMETHING TO TRY: Look for a building or a row of buildings, then draw a picture of what you see. Follow the rules for drawing the lines as described above.

Draw a picture of buildings or other cubed objects such as vehicles. You decide!

Final Project
Lesson 4

Application

Student Gallery

Student work is by Naomi Kerley.

Student work on top by Aaron Garrison.

YOU WILL NEED

- colored pencil set
- sketch paper
- vinyl eraser

THE SUBJECT

Choose one of these subjects for your drawing.
- Houses in your neighborhood
- A city street
- A painting (the Impressionists liked to paint street scenes)
- A four wheeled vehicle

LOOK BACK! Are the vertical lines in your drawing parallel with the sides of the paper? Are the horizontal lines in your drawing parallel with the top and bottom of the paper? Imagine a cube around your object. Are the diagonal lines on any one cube parallel with each other?

Lesson 1

unit 14
Figure

Vocabulary and Creative Exercise

A figure is the term artists use to talk about the entire body from head to toe. Figures are a favorite subject for artists to draw and paint. Once you know more about proportion you can give your figures movement like the figures above.

using creativity

A football player understands the impact of a tackle better than a fan who watches. The fan only sees with the eyes. The player sees, acts, hears, and feels. Because of this, the football player has a fuller experience. An artist who wants to draw an activity may want to participate in it first. Then the artist can fully experience what he draws. A deeper awareness of an object or scene comes from the artist's participation in it.

TRY IT: Think of a physical activity that requires you to move your whole body. Ballet, sports, walking, and swimming are such activities. Act out the activity. Feel where the body bends, twists, stretches, and pulls. You will become more aware of the motion, which will help you draw a figure in motion. Draw a picture of the way the body moves.

OBJECTIVE: to develop awareness of the body in action and translate that into a drawing.

Look at the Figure in Art   Lesson 2

Art Appreciation

N.C. Wyeth (1882-1944) *Above the Sea of Round, Shiny Backs the Thin Loops Swirled and Shot into Volumes of Dust*, 1904. Oil on canvas. 38 ¼ x 26 in. Photo Credit: Dover Publications, Inc. NY

The figure in this painting leans forward. His right leg catches the weight of his movement. We can imagine his right arm swinging outward within moments in order to lasso a horse as the herd of horses passes him up. Figures look different from various angles and are fairly complex to draw. As you draw more figures, these complexities become more familiar and are more easily put on paper. You will have the opportunity to search out the proportions of a figure in this lesson.

THE ARTIST:
N.C. Wyeth (1882-1944) Illustrator and Artist

N. C. Wyeth had a rich family history. His relatives fought in all the American wars and enjoyed telling first hand stories of their experiences. His mother knew several famous literary geniuses of the time. Wyeth enjoyed costumes and used a variety of them to cloth the models who posed for his paintings. He sold his first artwork at age 21 and got a second commission for a book on the West. To prepare for the novel, he traveled to the state of Colorado where he acquired direct knowledge of the Western lifestyle. He worked as a cowboy with professional punchers, moving cattle and doing ranch chores. After creating many paintings of his Western experience, Wyeth moved on to paint illustrations for classical literature. His best known illustrations are for a book edition of *Treasure Island* by Robert Louis Stevenson. Wyeth stated, "If you paint a man leaning over, your own back must ache." He showed this idea by example, going to the places and setting up the scenes for each of his illustrations. This brought the kind of reality to his paintings that helped people visualize the story.

THE TIMES:

As you study the art of America it becomes clear that America is a diverse nation. At times people come together with common goals that define artistic movements. At other times artists strive to be individuals with completely unique ideas. Early in America's brief history, nearly all artists traveled to Europe to further their education and see the works of the great masters where art had been created for millennia (thousands of years). Artists relied heavily on the tutorship of older artists, first meeting in homes and studios and later in established colleges throughout the United States. This tradition was followed until the early part of the 20th century when European wars drove artists to leave their countries and make new homes in America. The freedom of thought and action that Americans enjoyed became a fertile ground for ideas and creativity to grow. America became the new center for art. Artist colonies and schools grew rapidly. Today we see a variety of works in abstract, realistic, and traditional methods of the native people. The art of America is as diverse as the people who live in it.

MAKE AN OBSERVATION DRAWING! Lay a piece of tracing paper over the figure on the previous page. Trace around the edges of the figure. Find other figures and do the same. Practice like this can help one to see figures in more realistic ways, with correct proportions. You may realize common errors in your figure drawings such as making the head too big or making the arms or legs too short. Once you complete the exercise you will be ready to draw any figure more accurately from observation.

Lesson 3
How to Draw the Figure

Measure the head from top to chin, and then find other similar measurements such as shoulder blades to waist and waist to crotch.

To make a figure with all parts in proportion to each other, check the following items.

The elbows should reach the waist.

Sometimes people forget to draw the stomach (between the waist and the crotch). Notice that this area is as long as the chest from waist to shoulder.

The arms should reach mid-thigh at the fingertips when at one's side.

Distance from the crotch to knees = distance from the knees to ankles.

SOMETHING TO TRY: Look at the figure on the right. Draw a similar kind of figure and try to keep the proportions correct. Keep proportions in mind even when bending legs and arms.

Techniques

Figures are difficult to draw from direct observation because we don't usually have a model to sit very still for us so that we can take the kinds of measurements shown on the previous page. You may want to make use of photographs that catch people in a pose that is both interesting and shows movement.

Make a full-color figure drawing using a photograph as a visual reference. First draw the outline and then details. Finally, fill in color areas. Use a variety of colors.

Final Project Lesson 4

Application

Student Gallery

These student works by Lavender Huskey were drawn using the sports section of the local newspaper as a photo reference.

YOU WILL NEED

- colored pencil set
- vinyl eraser
- drawing paper

THE SUBJECT

Draw a figure from a photograph or life. Look in

- Newspapers
- Magazines
- Calendars

LOOK BACK! What do you like about your figure drawing? Do the arms look long enough? Do the legs look long enough? Does the head look too large or too small? Do not be critical of the results. These questions just help you to focus on those particular parts of the figure.

Lesson 1

unit 15
Faces

Vocabulary and Creative Exercise

When putting the face on paper it is important to see it as one object, not a bunch of separate features such as eyes, nose, mouth, and ears. A face is more similar in form to an egg than it is to a ball, so we have used an egg as a model. A line is drawn at midpoint for the eyes. The nose line is drawn half-way from the eye line to the chin. The mouth line is drawn halfway between the nose line and chin. The model can then be tilted in any direction and it gives you a good idea of where to place the individual features.

using creativity

The best way to get a good idea is to have lots of ideas. When making art, do not stop with your first idea. Instead, sketch many ideas on paper. Then, look at them and ask which designs look best, what do I like about it, and what you could change to make it better. Don't stop with the first solution. Explore many solutions and make changes.

TRY IT: Boil an egg. Let it cool and dry. With a colored pencil, draw lines, as shown above, all the way around the egg. Draw the features. Notice that the line for the eyes is in the middle of the egg. Turn the egg in different directions and draw the facial features using the egg as a model. Try many possibilities. Add hair, ears, and more to your drawings.

OBJECTIVE: to explore many different options using observation of a model.

Look at Faces in Art   Lesson 2

In Europe, paintings were reserved for nobles who dressed in fine and fancy clothing. Early American portrait painting has a unique feature. Artists boldly painted the people around them in the common dress of the day. This boy is in a common shirt and jacket. His hat is torn. The artist, Thomas Sully, renders the picture as carefully as any fine painting would be painted. The boy stares at the artist directly. His character is typical of the new confidence that grew as a result of living in a free society where all men are created equal.

Thomas Sully 1783-1872. *Boy with a Yellow Hat*, Photo Credit: Dover Publications Inc.

When drawing faces, the most common mistake is to place the eyes too high, even when told that the eyes should rest between the top of the head and the chin. The reason for this is that we confuse the hairline with the top of the head. The hairline falls somewhere between the eyes and top of the head. The location of the hairline varies greatly, so you have to observe each individual. Here, the top of the head is hidden by the hat. When located, the eyes fall right into place, as shown in the diagram.

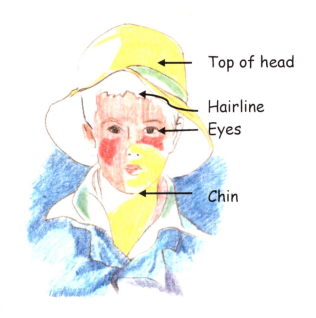

THE ARTIST:
Thomas Sully (1783-1872)
American Artist

Thomas Sully was born in England. He moved to America when he was nine years old. Sully began to study painting at about twelve years of age. As a young man, he settled in Philadelphia where he painted portraits of people. His favorite subject was always people. He is known for brilliant lighting and fine brushwork. Sully made many elegant portraits of important people living just after the American Revolution. Fine portrait painters like Sully, who could paint in the realistic manner of the English nobility painters, gave credibility to young American generals and patriots of the American Revolution. These now famous men and women appeared like nobility to the viewing eyes of the people living in America.

MAKE AN OBSERVATION DRAWING!

In this self portrait choose to wear a favorite hat or accessory that tells something about you tastes or things you like. You may wear a shirt with a sports team logo, a favorite fun hat, or other article of clothing around the face, neck, or chest.

THE TIMES:

In the eighteenth century there were no photographs. Images of people were not common. Only a prosperous person could afford to hire an artist to paint a portrait. A portrait preserved the image of the person. A portrait can tell us what a person looked like, as well as showing us how important the person was. The first settlers were familiar with portrait paintings of European nobles. But America was not made up of nobles with inherited wealth. The early settlers were common men who earned their wealth through hard work. They desired to imitate the wealthy noble lifestyle of England in their homes, furniture, and portraits. Early portrait painters in America could earn a fine living if they were able to create an image that looked like the person. The common man of America was painted in the same way and with the same techniques as a noble from Europe. This elevated the importance of the common man. During the American Revolution a new generation of artists rose up and produced portraits that glorified the independent nature of the Revolutionary hero and his family. Many paintings of statesmen, war heroes, and political figures of the new nation were made to honor these men who were great because of their deeds, not because of their ancestry. George Washington sat still to have his portrait painted by at least nineteen different artists and several sculptors during his lifetime. Early American history was well recorded by early American portrait painters of the time. They provided many pictures of the heroes who founded our nation.

Lesson 3

How to Draw the Parts of a Face

When you look at the illustrations below, do not just copy them. Use them to see how the features of the face are built. Then study your own face or the face of another person. Once you understand how the face is constructed make the adjustments so that each feature looks like the ones on the person you are drawing.

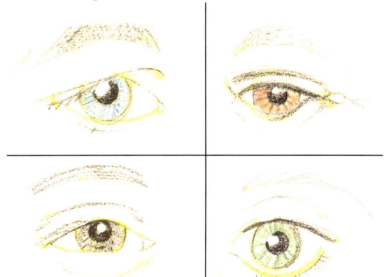

THE EYE

The eye ball is a complete circle, a ball set in a socket. The opening does not allow us to see the entire ball. How the skin lays around the eye is part of what makes each person unique. Look at the variety of openings and lid shapes in just the four examples at the right.

THE NOSE AND LIPS

Noses and lips are as individual as eyes. Shapes of the nostrils and the contour from the side vary greatly from person to person. It is important to keep in mind that some lines are distinct while others require a lighter touch with the pencil.

← Subtle shading →

Strong line

Subtle shading
Strong line
Subtle shading

SOMETHING TO TRY: Make a drawing of your own eyes as you see them in a mirror. Later you might want to practice drawing features of different people within your household or of your friends. People have differently shaped noses, eyes, and mouths. Look for the differences.

Final Project Lesson 4

On a sheet of paper draw a self portrait. Look in a mirror to get a good look at yourself. Draw your features as you see them. Start with the egg shape as shown in lesson one of this unit. Place eyes halfway between the top of the head and the chin. Place the nose halfway between the eyes and chin, and place the mouth halfway between the nose and the chin. Place objects in the background that tell about something you like.

Student Gallery

Student work below is by Vincent Darger.
Student work at the right is by Geoffrey Lohr.

Each work shows good placement of the eyes and other important facial features.

YOU WILL NEED

- colored pencil set
- vinyl eraser
- drawing paper

THE SUBJECT

The subject is you. Set up a mirror and your drawing materials so that you can look at yourself directly with a front viewpoint.

LOOK BACK! In what ways does your drawing look like you? A likeness means that the features look enough like a person that they could be identified by your drawing. It is not like a photo. Did you create a likeness?

Lesson 1

unit 16
Interiors

Vocabulary and Creative Exercise

 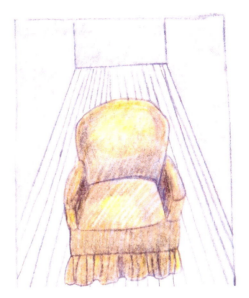

An interior can be made by arranging sets of parallel lines so that they appear to converge at the distant end of the room. A wall is created by placing a vertical line on the converging lines. Erase lines behind the wall.

using creativity

Creativity is best observed in those people who take an interest in many areas of life. Real objects and real experiences are like food to the creative mind. They feed it and it grows. You can test this idea by comparing two drawings, one drawn from your imagination and one drawn by observing and experiencing an object.

TRY IT: First draw a shoe, without looking at one. Next go to a closet to observe a variety of shoes. Pick some up and notice buttons, heels, texture, size, laces, etc. Now select the shoe that you find most interesting. Set it on the table to observe it as you draw the details in the second drawing. Finally, compare the two pictures. After your experience with shoes, did it help you draw a better or more interesting shoe?

OBJECTIVE: to better understand the benefits of using experience and direct observation in creating artwork.

Look at an Interior in Art   Lesson 2

Art Appreciation

Colin Campbell Cooper, *Cottage Interior*, n.d.
Photo Credit: Dover Publications Inc.

This interior is filled with furniture. Furniture is usually a combination of cubes and cylinders, altered at times by curving lines. You can draw more accurately when you see what basic forms a piece of furniture is made up of.

Cube
Cylinder

87

THE ARTIST:
Colin Campbell Cooper (1856-1937)
American Impressionist Painter

Colin Campbell Cooper was encouraged to become an artist by his parents. He enrolled in the Pennsylvania Academy of Fine Arts, and was a student of Thomas Eakins. He then studied in Europe, as many artists did when they could afford it. He traveled throughout Europe and continued to travel often during his lifetime. He was on the *S.S. Carpathia,* making a leisurely passage to the Mediterranean from New York, when it came to the rescue of passengers on the sinking *Titanic*. He made paintings of the rescue while on board the ship. Cooper lived on the West Coast but kept a residence in New York as well. His Impressionistic paintings were well liked and he was especially noted for paintings of buildings in New York City.

MAKE AN OBSERVATION DRAWING!

Find a cube. Light the cube from one side. Draw the cube. Change the angle and draw it again. Draw it from many angles.

THE TIMES:

Travel in the early 1800's was slow and land travel in the United States was limited to stage coaches and wagons drawn by oxen or horses. By the late 1800's much had changed. New inventions made ocean and land travel faster. The beginning of the big ship era started in 1907 as the *Adriatic II* departed from Southampton, England to make a transatlantic voyage to the United States. These Ocean Liners could make a trip from Europe to America in about one week. The largest and most luxurious Ocean liner was the *Titanic*. On its first voyage it tragically struck an iceberg and sank rapidly on April 14, 1912. The events of the sinking Titanic shocked the world.

The transcontinental railroad was newly completed in November of 1869, just 40 years before the Titanic sank. Traveling from the east coast to the west coast by land had taken Lewis and Clark two and a half years. By train it now took nine days! Cooper boarded these new trains to get from his home in New York to California. At the time of his birth, these modern transportation systems were non-existent. He must have felt very proud to travel in such style. New systems of transportation meant that he could make art from locations all over the world. And that is what he did.

Lesson 3

How to Draw Cylinders and Cubes

Here we show a few furniture shapes that rely strongly on the forms of cube and cylinder.

CUBE

CYLINDER

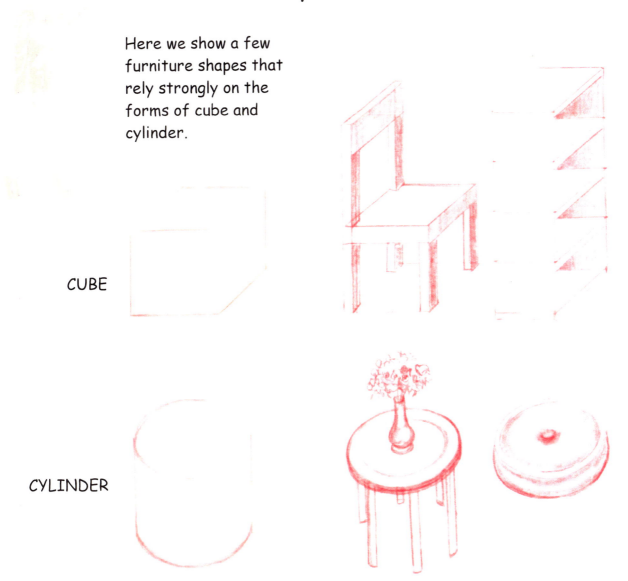

On the cube and the cylinder the vertical lines always stay parallel to the sides of the paper. Diagonal lines on a single cube remain at the same angle.

Look at the legs of the chair and table. Drawing the entire simplified shape, including the bottom, helps to tell you where the legs should end. Draw these lines, then erase later.

SOMETHING TO TRY: Find objects in your own home that have strong cube or cylinder forms. Draw the simplified form in light lines. Then draw the object over it in darker lines.

Make a full color painting of an interior space using watercolor pencils. The interior space may include objects that move around within that space.

Final Project
Lesson 4

Application

Student Gallery

Student work above by Amy Wright uses all inanimate objects. Student work below by Lavender Huskey includes a cat and dog.

YOU WILL NEED

- watercolor pencils
- watercolor brush
- watercolor paper
- water container
- masking tape
- paper towels

THE SUBJECT

An interior may include objects that are not alive (those that remain in the room permanently) or objects that are alive (those people or animals that move from one place to another).

LOOK BACK! Did you think about which subjects to include in the interior scene? Does your scene include objects that move around or objects that are stationary?

Evaluation Sheet
FOR OBTAINING A NUMBER AND LETTER GRADE

Teachers may calculate a number and letter grade for each project within each unit. Follow the instructions below as you look at the final work. DO NOT take off points for concepts not yet taught. Follow the objectives carefully when grading.

Because of art's subjective qualities it is best to mark higher rather than lower when deciding between two levels of achievement. If the student enjoyed doing the lessons and has made the effort to create a work of art in a thoughtful way, then that student should be given a good grade. Allow the student to grow into mature artistic expression. Do not demand results that can only be obtained by repeated experience that the student has not yet had. It is very likely that an individual who enjoys making art will get A's. This does not mean that the student has arrived at a full knowledge and use of artistic concepts. It does mean the student is doing well in the pursuit of that goal.

LEVELS OF ACHIEVEMENT Choose the number of points, which most accurately describes the work from each of the three options below. Add the numbers from categories 1, 2, 3, and 4. This is the student's total score for the unit. This number can be translated into a letter grade: 90-100 (A) 80-89 (B) 70-79 (C) Incomplete work (D-F).

Note: If you do not see how the student accomplished the objectives asked for, **do ask them about it**. Sometimes they understood very well and will be able to tell you how they accomplished the task in the drawing. This is valid. Remember that getting a visual idea across clearly is a process that takes time. Allow the student to grow into it.

1. Using Creativity	2. Make a Drawing	3. Something to Try	4. Final Project
25 POINTS/ COMPLETED ASSIGNMENT AND OBTAINED ALL OBJECTIVES IN BLUE BOX AT THE BOTTOM OF THE PAGE	25 POINTS/ COMPLETED ASSIGNMENT IN BLUE SHOWS GOOD UNDERSTANDING OF CONCEPT SHOWN IN ART WORK	25 POINTS/ COMPLETED ASSIGNMENT IN BLUE SHOWS GOOD UNDERSTANDING AND USE OF MATERIALS OR TECHNIQUES	25 POINTS/ COMPLETED PROJECT SHOWS GOOD UNDERSTANDING OF THE UNIT (SEE TITLE) AND USE OF THOSE ITEMS ASKED FOR IN THE GREEN BOX AT THE BOTTOM OF THE PAGE
20 POINTS/ COMPLETED ASSIGNMENT AND OBTAINED SOME OF THE OBJECTIVES IN BLUE BOX AT THE BOTTOM OF THE PAGE	20 POINTS/ COMPLETED ASSIGNMENT IN BLUE SHOWS AN ATTEMPT TO USE CONCEPT SHOWN IN ART WORK	20 POINTS/ COMPLETED ASSIGNMENT IN BLUE SHOWS AN ATTEMPT TO USE MATERIALS OR TECHNIQUES	20 POINTS/ COMPLETED PROJECT SHOWS UNDERSTANDING OF UNIT BUT DID NOT ACCOMPLISH SOME ITEMS ASKED FOR IN THE GREEN BOX AT THE BOTTOM OF THE PAGE
15 POINTS/ COMPLETED ASSIGNMENT BUT DID NOT OBTAIN OBJECTIVES IN THE BLUE BOX AT THE BOTTOM OF THE PAGE	15 POINTS/ COMPLETED ASSIGNMENT IN BLUE DID NOT USE CONCEPT SHOWN IN ART WORK	15 POINTS/ COMPLETED ASSIGNMENT IN BLUE DID NOT USE MATERIALS CORRECTLY OR TRY THE TECHNIQUE SHOWN	15 POINTS/ COMPLETED PROJECT DID NOT SHOW UNDERSTANDING OF UNIT OR ITEMS IN GREEN BOX AT THE BOTTOM OF THE PAGE

Bibliography

Batterberry, Ariane Ruskin and Michael. *The Pantheon Story of American Art for Young People*. Pantheon Books, 1976.

Chotner, Deborah. *American Naïve Paintings*. Oxford University Press, 1983.

Sloan, John. *Gist of Art*. Recorded by Helen Farr. 1939.

The Collection, National Gallery of Art. http://www.nga.gov/cgi-bin/pinfo?Object=39456+0+none Retrieved Jan. 1, 2008.

Wheelwright Museum of the American Indian. http://www.wheelwright.org/about.html. Retrieved Oct. 29, 2012.

Wright, Tricia. *American Art and Artists, Smithsonian Q&A*. Hydra Publishing, 2007.